PRAISE FOR
You Got This!

"Lisa Bartley's fabulous book, *You Got This!* is filled with gems. Treasures. I can't recommend it highly enough. Brava, brava, brava! Truly wonderful."

—Amy Ferris, screenwriter, playwright, and author of *Mighty Gorgeous: A Little Book About Messy Love*

"Lisa Bartley has written the book I wish I'd had in my twenties—a refreshingly honest guide that tackles the messy realities of growing up without sugarcoating the hard parts."

—Pat Henneberry, bestselling author of *My Soul Showed Up: Finding Hope and Resilience Against All Odds*

"*You Got This!* is like having a smart, supportive friend remind you that you're capable of so much more than you realize—and then giving you the exact steps to make it happen."

—Nancy Mae Johnson, author of *Things My Mama Never Told Me*

you got this!

HONEST LESSONS *on* LIFE,
LOVE, *and* LEVELING UP

LISA BARTLEY

Helping talented writers publish exceptional books

You Got This! Honest Lessons on Life, Love, and Leveling Up

For my daughter, Madison.
I hope you make the best choices I ever made
. . . and the best choices I never made.

INTRODUCTION

It takes a village to raise a child. A village to nurture a teenager. And a village to cheer them on throughout adulthood. Yet, in recent decades, that village has practically become extinct. Economic pressures have left families feeling overworked, overwhelmed, and overstressed with little time and energy to support and cheer on the next generation of powerhouse women—leaders, creatives, rock star moms, trailblazers, and community enthusiasts. Digital communication has replaced face-to-face interaction. And while social media may give the illusion of connection, it doesn't offer the same wholehearted encouragement, wisdom, and insight that communal and multigenerational relationships once did. And then there are those who feel isolated due to relocation, depression, divorce, and tragic loss. Where's their tight-knit tribe? And who can they look to when facing important—and sometimes life-altering—choices?

The landscape of the proverbial village has changed, and the shift has left a hollow space—one that begs to be filled. Consider the following:

- Women today have more career opportunities than ever before . . . but less of a village to help them seize those opportunities confidently and assertively, without second-guessing themselves.
- We're feeling more empowered to pursue our passions . . . but have less of a grassroots cheering squad shouting, "You Got This!" from the sidelines.
- We're encouraged to lean in . . . but we're hearing fewer communal and societal words of wisdom when we miss the mark—a community rallying around us, reminding us that strike three doesn't mean we're out.

This good news–bad news dichotomy raises the question, *Where can women find support and sage advice when navigating the decisions, the triumphs, the hurdles, the self-doubt, and the ebb and flow of early-to-mid adulthood?*

The village has shrunk, while the need for it has expanded.

You Got This! Honest Lessons on Life, Love, and Leveling Up is *my* contribution to the diminishing village. After coaching thousands of people over the past fifteen years, raising a son and daughter, and yes, having the perspective of seeing my own twenties and thirties in the rearview mirror, I've gained insights that—if time travel were possible—I would have excitedly shared with my younger self. Instead, I'm sharing them with *you.*

Originally intended as a literary blueprint for my daughter, Madison, I started jotting down bullet-pointed life lessons. Some of those lessons I learned the easy way, some the hard way, and others by simply observing the cause and effect that played out among friends and family. As a mom, I felt a deep desire to help my daughter make smart choices; to give her the benefit of everything I had done right as well as the benefit of everything . . . Well, let's just say everything I would have done differently, had there been a do-over. I also wanted to bequeath maternal words of wisdom from my mom, Norma, and her mom, Grandma Libby. Sure, societal norms have changed over the years. But human nature has *not*. This would be a gift—*my* gift—to my daughter.

I continued to scribble down thoughts, mentally fast-forwarding to the time when these insights would have the greatest impact on the trajectory of her life. One day, I realized this "gift" had book potential. Women just like you—in the throes of life-defining decisions—could benefit from practical generational guidance, along with the assurance, *You Got This!*

The pages that follow have been a work in progress for over twenty years and therefore the content has evolved over time. Let me explain. In my role as a personal and professional development coach and trainer, I've had the privilege of helping men and women across all walks of life uncover blind spots, overcome challenges, and close the gap between *who* they are now and *who* they want to be. And I say "who" they are and "who" they want to be instead of "where" they are and "where" they want to be because we can only alter where we're going by first recognizing and adjusting *who* we're being; who we're showing up as in our day-to-day lives. It's always exciting to see the transformation! The thrill of being part of that process never gets old. Bolstered by their newfound confidence, clients have made bolder moves, improved the quality of their relationships, and become the architects of their own lives. I'm excited and honored to help you do the same!

Interestingly, throughout the years, some patterns began to emerge, especially among my *female* coaching clients and workshop participants. As they articulated their goals and visions—along with their fears and frustrations—it became clear that the Five Pillars of Empowerment™ were necessary to support their dreams and aspirations: Self-Confidence, Courage, Assertiveness, Resilience, and Self-Acceptance. Courage, as I define it here, is the willingness to acknowledge your worth, step out of your comfort zone, take risks, and pursue your passions.

As I was refining *You Got This!* and developing the Action Steps for each chapter, I began to intertwine the Five Pillars of Empowerment with some of the biggest challenges women are facing in their twenties and thirties: dating; self-respect; setting boundaries; relationships with friends, family, and colleagues; learning from life's disappointments; following their dreams; and reaching their full potential.

While each vignette-style chapter focuses on a life lesson in one of those areas, the chapters are also designed to help you build one or more (usually more!) of the Five Pillars of Empowerment. Again, they are Self-Confidence, Courage, Assertiveness, Resilience, and Self-Acceptance. To help you remember these pillars and establish a benchmark to review and measure your progress, I've developed the acronym SCARS, as in the battle SCARS we invariably and proudly develop as we step into the arena, à la Brené Brown, and play full out!

In Part One: The Dating Game, I'll share practical advice like "Avoid the Tendency to Overcompensate for Previous Relationship Flaws" and "Don't Date Sprinters If You're Looking for a Long-Distance Runner." In the life lesson, "Love is Like Being in a Boxing Ring," you'll discover you can't guard your heart and leave it open at the same time, along with strategies to help you "get back in the ring."

One of the biggest decisions you will ever make is choosing a life partner. In fact, studies show that fulfilling relationships lead to higher levels of happiness. And the choice of a life partner has a profound effect on a person's overall quality of life. Yet, many women find the right one to be elusive. That's why The Dating Game is its own section and includes pitfalls to watch out for; warning signs, many of which others did not consider. Even if you're already married,

I hope you'll still read through this section. I promise there will be something helpful and entertaining you can share with your single friends and relatives.

In some ways, *You Got This!* evolves right along with you.

Part Two: Respect Yourself/Setting Boundaries/Kindred Spirits focuses on themes that set a foundation for fulfillment and future success. You'll build confidence as you find your voice in the thick of unfamiliar or uncomfortable conversations. For example, in chapter 27, "Confrontation Doesn't Have to Be Confrontational," I share a six-step process to help you assertively and fearlessly navigate an otherwise difficult exchange. You'll also learn in chapter 23 why "Invisible Boundaries Are Worse than No Boundaries at All." And if you're struggling to forgive someone, I'll explain why forgiveness is not simply a gift you give the other person, but one you give yourself.

The three themes in Part Two are interrelated. Self-respect is the value we place on ourselves. And the boundaries we set —or fail to set—reflect that value. Both are foundational to building and maintaining "kindred spirits" with our friends, family, and colleagues. There's an abundance of research correlating clear boundaries with confidence, personal growth, mutual respect, career advancement, mental health, and lower levels of stress and anxiety. According to one study in *The Journal of Positive Psychology*, women who set clear boundaries have better coping strategies and can navigate difficult situations more effectively.

Among the biggest regrets people report later in life is not having reached their full potential or not having pursued their passions when they were younger. Part Three: Strike Three Doesn't Mean You're Out/Follow Your Dreams/Step Into the Best Version of You is all about reaching your full potential in spite of—and sometimes *because* of—hurdles and disappointments along the way. In "Run Your Own Race," I encourage you to compete against yourself instead of competing against others. One approach encourages continuous growth and the other tugs on your insecurities. In "Accountability Makes No Excuses," you'll find there are varying degrees of accountability and why choosing the top tier is really the only option if you want to elevate your relationships and your reputation. In the life lesson, "We See Exactly What We're Looking For," we'll explore the concept of Intentional Perspective and the importance of adjusting the lens through which we view relationships, work, and opportunities.

While I certainly offer plenty of tips and advice, I also pose lots of questions designed to help you take a deeper dive into your choices and the motivation behind them. Questions that build your critical thinking muscle so that your personal development journey extends far beyond the pages of this book. Questions to inspire you to be the best possible version of yourself . . . and to empower you to support and mentor other women to do the same.

What you can expect from this book: a series of lightbulb moments, sparked by stories, insights, tips, and strategies to help you claim the life, the love, the respect, and the opportunities you want and deserve.

What *not* to expect: While there are many noteworthy books that explore religious, political, and social issues, I've chosen to focus on topics that unite, rather than divide, us. That being said, most of the Action Steps in each chapter can be applied to a variety of situations.

Although much of the content in this book is relevant to men, it has been written with a female audience in mind. I hope to foster a spirit of women helping women. We need each other. We need the village. And while you're not *my* daughter, you are *someone's* daughter. And that's reason enough for me to want to contribute to you in a meaningful way.

I'm grateful you've chosen to invest in this book, and more importantly, that you've chosen to invest in yourself. Throughout the pages that follow, I'll share forty-six micro life lessons along with no-nonsense Action Steps to help you put insights and advice into practice. Names (and sometimes details) have been changed to protect the innocent . . . *and the guilty.* Although *You Got This!* can be a solo journey, please consider reading this with a friend, or even an "accountabili-buddy." Supporting each other and exchanging experiences, past and present, will help you to see your growth, and your life, as a journey instead of a checklist. Besides, everything's better when we share it with someone—except, maybe, that last serving of Häagen-Dazs Vanilla Swiss Almond!

I'm rooting for you to lean in. To claim your seat at the table—whether that's the conference table, the kitchen table, the negotiations table, or the round table. I'm rooting for you to come into your own and step into the best version of your-self with confidence, optimism, and the unwavering belief that *You Got This!*

PART ONE

THE DATING GAME

AVOID THE TENDENCY TO OVERCOMPENSATE FOR PREVIOUS RELATIONSHIP FLAWS

Everyone loved Robert. He was fun. Loyal. Sincere. And did I mention gorgeous? He was one of those guys who could instantly put anyone at ease. Robert had been dating Grace for the past three years. Everyone was certain they would eventually get married—that is, everyone but *Grace*.

He was a catch, but she had her reservations. "He just doesn't have enough drive," she told me one day. "He's really smart. He has so much going for him, but he just doesn't have any goals."

Grace ended her three-year relationship and within weeks she was dating Charlie—a real go-getter. *Hmm . . . interesting.* What made Charlie so irresistible was the elusive quality that Robert lacked: professional drive. He was quickly moving up the corporate ladder, garnering the respect and admiration of coworkers and senior-level executives. Like Robert, Charlie was also a great guy . . . if only he didn't have three kids.

Fresh out of college and on the heels of a promising career, Grace wasn't ready to be a full-time mother.

After a year with Charlie, things fizzled because Grace had focused on one characteristic to the exclusion of other traits and circumstances that were also important to her. In short, she overcompensated. By placing so much emphasis on ambition, she failed to see the whole picture, including a ready-made family that she wasn't prepared to take on. It was no surprise, then, when Grace started dating Jackson, a confirmed bachelor who didn't see kids in the picture for many, many years to come.

And so, the pendulum swings.

Grace's pattern is a common one. We tend to overcompensate for previous relationship flaws by dating or marrying someone who offers what the last person did not. We want what was missing and naturally gravitate toward it. That's understandable. But if you focus on one thing so intently, you may lose track of everything else. Instead, take a step back. Look at the whole picture. Know what's important to you—*all* of it.

Sadly, Grace paid the price for overcompensating. She eventually married Jackson and soon discovered there was a reason he couldn't imagine kids in the foreseeable future. He didn't know how to be faithful, and kids would have seriously interfered with his "extracurricular activities." Thankfully, Grace *found* out and *got* out. Having gone through several rounds of "overcompensating," she evaluated her dating pattern, looked at her relationships more holistically, and broke the cycle.

With each relationship, we grow. We learn a little bit more about who we are and what we want. If we can *factor in* previous relationship flaws, rather than *overcompensate* for them, it will bring us closer to finding our ideal match.

ACTION STEP:

- Write down the ten qualities that are most important to you in a long-term romantic relationship. Eliminate one trait at a time until you get to your top three. These are likely your deal-breakers. If the relationship pendulum swings too far in one direction, this will help you refocus and bring you back to center. Back to what's truly important to you.

DON'T DATE SPRINTERS IF YOU'RE LOOKING FOR A LONG-DISTANCE RUNNER

I f so many women are looking for Mr. Right, why are so many out on Saturday night with Mr. Wrong? The answers are endless, but here's one that covers a lot of ground: Some women date Sprinters when they really want a Long-Distance Runner.

Sprinters—you know the type. They're charming. Charismatic. And *so* into you. They make a great first impression. But, of course they do. They exert a lot of energy at the *beginning* of the relationship. Always attentive, they say and do all the right things, convincing you that this could be "it." Naturally, you assume things can only get better. But these guys never quite go the distance. They're not wired that way. They're Sprinters. Not Long-Distance Runners. You're just warming up, and they're already looking for another finish line!

The truth is, most women don't realize they're with a Sprinter until he's long gone, leaving nothing behind but emotional skid marks and an unanswered text. So here are a few clues that the sprint is over but he still wants to linger on the track:

- **Breadcrumbing.** He gives you just enough attention and communication to keep you interested in him, but not enough to move the relationship forward.
- **You're never quite sure where you stand.** He doesn't commit, and he keeps you guessing. More on this in chapter 13.
- **You feel like a well-kept secret.** He wants to get together at his place. Or at your place. But not necessarily in a *public* place.
- **He doesn't like talking about the future.** And by "future," I'm not simply referring to the M-word. When you bring up holidays, travel, or even plans a couple of months out, he feels like you're coming on too strong or "getting ahead of yourself." This is a major tell that he's in it for the sprint, not the marathon.
- **He's dating a rush, not a relationship.** He's comfortable with physical closeness, but not emotional intimacy. He creates an emotional rush to lower your guard—not to build a bond. To him, it's not about connection. It's about momentum . . . toward the bedroom.

Being a Sprinter doesn't make him a bad person. It just means if you want something more sustainable, he's probably not the right person for *you*—at least at this point in time. You see, the Sprinter doesn't typically encounter any bumps in the road. He runs a fast and furious race. When it's over, he can only capture that same level of excitement by starting—*and finishing*—with someone else. So if that unbelievably perfect guy lost interest in you after the three most amazing months of your life, with no logical explanation in sight, don't lose too much sleep trying to figure out what went wrong. He was probably a Sprinter.

On the other hand, the Long-Distance Runner actually enjoys a longer journey. He's built to last. He knows there will be obstacles along the way. He accepts this. He anticipates it. And he is prepared for the difficulties that lie ahead. From the start, he realizes he may feel like throwing in the towel, but because he loves you and is in it for the long haul, he rises above challenges like health issues, financial problems, and differences in communication styles. He's a one-woman man who isn't afraid of love and commitment.

I know, I know. Sprinters make a woman's heart race! Truth be told, they can be much more exciting than Long-Distance Runners. But you get to a point when you realize that there is more to life than excitement. There comes a time when you're ready for something more. Trust. Longevity. Real intimacy. A soft place to fall. I'm not saying that your only option is to settle down with Eugene in accounting. Chemistry and trustworthiness are not mutually exclusive.

If you're ready for a long-term commitment, determine what kind of runner this guy is. Ask yourself: *Does he really love me? Are we best friends? If we want children one day, what kind of father will he be? Will he put our family ahead of everyone and everything else? Is he a man of honor? How does he handle conflict? Does he have the grit—the perseverance, determination, and intestinal fortitude—to withstand life's adversities; to stay focused on the long-term goal of building a life together? When it comes to challenges, is he proactive or reactive? Is he someone who gets up and brushes himself off after he falls down?* The answers will tell you if he is a 100-yard-dash kind of guy or a Boston Marathon man. If you're dating a Sprinter and he's getting what *he* wants out of the relationship and you're not, someone is going to get hurt. You do the math!

ACTION STEPS:

- As you revisit these questions, do you think your partner is a Sprinter or a Long-Distance Runner? If it's looking like he's a Sprinter, are you okay with that? No judgment here. I'm simply pointing out that we want our choices to align with our desired outcomes.

- Reflect on the following questions: If you have a pattern of dating Sprinters, is that working for you? Or is it leaving you with feelings of self-doubt? Are you dating Sprinters because, when it comes down to it, *you* are the one who's afraid of making a commitment? If so, what's keeping you from going deeper with someone? Take an honest look at yourself. Sometimes we don't ask ourselves the hard questions because we already know we're not going to like the answers.

- If you decide you want to be with a Long-Distance Runner, then be the kind of woman a Long-Distance Runner is willing to "go the distance" for: Someone who deeply respects her man and deeply respects herself. That means setting some boundaries and having a certain level of independence. Don't simply be interested *in* him. Be interesting *to* him. And to yourself. Have your own life—people and hobbies and aspirations that light you up! While men (and women) like feeling special and love receiving accolades, a Long-Distance Runner worth his salt wants more than to simply be adored by you. He wants to be challenged, intrigued, loved, and understood. And though he wants to be the most important thing in

your life, he doesn't want to be the *only* thing in your life. That's a lot of pressure . . . for *any* man.
- Close your eyes. Picture yourself five years from now. Is he there? Fast-forward another ten years. How about now? Keep your eyes closed and imagine yourself at fifty. Do you see him? Is he next to you? Are you happy? What about seventy, or eighty? This is a quick litmus test, revealing innate wisdom that may have otherwise been difficult to access.

THREE

TRUE CHARACTER IS NOT REVEALED ON THE FIRST DATE

"It was love at first sight." So she thought.

When Jennifer first met Craig, she saw two things: what *he* chose to reveal and what *she* chose to see. *Come on. If he's charming and smokin' hot, do we really want to see the flaws?*

Three years later, Jennifer confessed, "He was surrounded by red flags, and I refused to see it."

In the end, Craig left her with a broken heart and a FICO score somewhere in the mid-500s. He guilt-tripped her into putting his new car and a couple of major credit cards in her name. At first, she said "no"—she knew it wasn't a good idea. But Craig wasn't the type to accept no for an answer, always insinuating, *if you really loved me . . .* He'd frame it like they were building something together—this was for *them*, for *their* future. When she still hesitated, he played the victim card and shifted emotional responsibility onto her: "Forget it then. I'll figure something else out." This wasn't surrender. It was bait. A carefully crafted manipulation to make Jennifer feel like she was abandoning *them*. And it worked. One repo and a dozen late payments later, the only thing she could afford to buy on credit was her cat.

But it didn't start with financial ruin. Everywhere they

went, people seemed drawn to Craig. Charismatic. Likable. Believable. Then came the slow erosion of her self-worth. Craig didn't raise his voice. He raised doubts by frequently gushing about other women's positive attributes—their talents, accomplishments, and stunning looks. He chipped away at her confidence with remarks like, "You have a stupid job. You'll never be anything." He knew she questioned her worth, so he played on that.

"I was at a low point in my life," Jennifer said to me. "I had just lost my job and had nowhere else to go. I told myself, *If I stay long enough, I can get back on my feet financially.* My head was saying, *Get out, Jen!* But I was feeling as if I would fall apart if I left."

Bottom line: True character is not revealed on the first date. How can it be? Life happens one day at a time. The challenges and adversities along the way—family difficulties, job changes, health issues, financial setbacks, personal losses, and our own demons—test *and expose* our character.

There's a turning point in every romance when we start "letting our mask slip." It usually happens about a year into the relationship. If we make a lifelong commitment prior to that, we may be signing up for habits and character flaws we're not even aware of. It's like we're signing a blank check—and we have no way of knowing what the ultimate price is going to be.

For Jennifer, it was very costly. Craig was, in her words, a "con man." He was manipulative and verbally abusive.

Their relationship had become toxic and codependent. But by then, her self-worth had been so thoroughly dismantled that leaving didn't feel like an option. Women who haven't been through this often ask, "Why didn't she just leave?" But when someone has spent months—even years—rewiring how you see yourself, leaving doesn't feel safe. As Jennifer put it, "When a controlling person tells you, 'You're nothing without me,' after a while, you start to believe them."

"Though I relied on him financially, he needed me too," she had assured herself. "I can fix him. I can show him something better than what he grew up around."

But that's not how Jennifer's story ended. He drained her bank account, along with her self-esteem and her dignity. Craig had nothing to offer Jennifer because he had nothing to offer himself. He was broken, and he was taking Jennifer down with him.

"I was at a crossroads," she recalls. "I'm either going to stay with him and spiral downward, or I'm going to start my life over."

She chose to be brave, and I'm so proud of her! The day she moved out—the day her internal switch finally flipped—their water had been turned off because Craig couldn't pay the bill. Jennifer walked out the door, glared over her shoulder, and with palpable disdain, said, "You can't even flush your own toilet, and you're calling *me* a loser?" She shut the door, literally and metaphorically, and never looked back.

Armed with newfound strength that was no longer being sapped by Craig, Jennifer *did* begin to build a new life for herself. Though she was uncertain about what lay ahead, she took steps in the right direction. She reconnected with what was most important to her and began surrounding herself with the right people—friends with similar values and priorities. She didn't have Craig in her head, planting seeds of doubt. There was now "white space" to fill with positive, joyful, and healthy thoughts. She could focus on goals and interests.

Jennifer eventually met a man she respected, fell in love with, and married. And what a catch! With eyes wide open, she was able to recognize not simply what she *wanted* to see, but what was truly there—*long after the first date.*

Time is your friend. Don't make long-term decisions based on fleeting impressions. Yes, I've seen whirlwind romances that have worked out; however, there are cards neither of you is showing. You're betting that he's holding a royal flush when he may not even have a pair . . . if you know what I mean.

When a relationship is fresh, *everyone* is on their best behavior. But people can only put their best foot forward for so long. Time reveals what needs to be revealed. It removes the flawless finish that we put on when we want to impress someone we really like. What's left beneath that carefully crafted exterior is raw character—and the person you could be spending the rest of your life with.

ACTION STEPS:

- In a casual way, ask a few of your boyfriend's family members, friends, or longtime colleagues, "What do you admire most about him?" Be sure to use the word "admire" or "respect." Asking what they "like" the most about him might garner responses that are more surface level, like, "He's the life of the party," which has its perks but won't necessarily tell you what you need to know.
- What did these conversations tell you? Were there any surprises? Did their replies shift your thinking in any way?

FOUR

IS HE ON THE REBOUND?

He's intelligent. He's thoughtful. He's so much fun.

Ugh. Figures. He's on the rebound.

Fresh off a two-year relationship, Mr. Wonderful is hot on your trail. Proceed with caution. He's been with someone for a while, so he's used to a few things. Lots of attention. Lots of girlfriend perks. And lots of sex. You might be six months into the relationship, and falling hard, before he realizes it's the comforts of a woman—not *you* in particular—that he's crazy about. *Ouch.*

True, sometimes all it takes is someone special (like you!) to make a guy realize what he's been missing out on all along. But, before you get in too deep, figure out if he's date-worthy and date-ready. Either by asking directly, or by allowing the answers to unfold organically in conversation, here's what you'll want to know:

Why did it end? If his last relationship went south when his girlfriend walked in on him with her best friend, my reaction would be much different than if it ended because he wanted to have children one day and she didn't. (Of course, not everyone will admit to the messier endings. But if the question makes him squirm, trust your gut.) Knowing *why* it ended will give you a glimpse into his character, values, and priorities.

Is he over her? He might *say* he is. And he may actually believe it. The answer may not be obvious to him (or you) because he's still trying to process and untangle his feelings about her. So be observant. Pay attention to subtleties. Be attuned to what he says about her—and what he doesn't say. Use your intuition. Be smart. Don't give your heart to someone who isn't ready to love you back. You may be the best thing that has ever happened to him, but he won't recognize or appreciate it if his heart is somewhere else. In the television series *Gilmore Girls*, did anyone really have a chance of winning Luke's heart when it had always belonged to Lorelai?

Was he married and did he take his vows seriously? When two people get married, they make a commitment to stay together "for better or for worse." If he walked out on his family because he wanted to dodge his responsibilities or if he filed for divorce before exploring every possible avenue for reconciliation, my antenna would go up. Yours should too.

Did *he* initiate the breakup? If so, he likely had time to process his thoughts and feelings, as well as grieve the loss of what once was, before cutting romantic ties. If it was *his* decision to call it quits, he's more likely to be ready to get involved than someone who just got dumped and has something to prove. A bruised ego can make a person rush into something he may not otherwise be ready for. Is his ego the one calling the shots?

Be cautious of the man on the rebound. He may need time to reflect on what wasn't working in his prior relationship and how he might have contributed to the breakup. He'll be in a better place after that.

Sure, sometimes it all works out in the end, but depending on the circumstances, he may be in a transitional phase. So ask yourself, *Would I rather be the girl who steals his heart, or just the one who temporarily helps him mend a broken one?*

ACTION STEP:

- It's important to know if he's the kind of man who learns from his experiences, or if he meanders through life, making the same mistakes over and over again. Self-awareness is a life skill, and it would be good to know where he lands on that continuum. Here's the question to ask anyone you're dating who has recently gone through a divorce or breakup: *If you had one do-over in your previous relationship, what would it be?* His response—and the *way* he responds—will tell you if he has grown as a result of the relationship and subsequent breakup. If he was the culpable party—and particularly if there was betrayal—his answer will either reveal remorse over his actions . . . or it won't.

FIVE

A MAN WHO INSISTS ON MOLDING YOU DOESN'T WANT A PARTNER—HE WANTS SOMEONE TO CONTROL

She was five-foot-three, 110 pounds. Her figure fit nicely into a pair of size 2 jeans. At nineteen, most guys liked the way she looked. But Lauren wasn't dating "most guys." She was dating someone who wanted to manipulate her. Someone who wanted to mold her into what he thought she should be. Someone who used the five-year age difference as a power play. All of this was his way of maintaining control.

"I'll buy you a new wardrobe," he announced one day, "if you can go from a size 2 jeans to a size 0." *Seriously? Talk about head games! A size 2 wasn't good enough? Thin enough?* Her hair was "too curly." He didn't like the wiggle in her walk. "It's a little girl's walk, not a woman's walk," he criticized. She was still a teenager. *What did he want, Jacqueline Kennedy Onassis?* He was impossible to please, but then again, that was all part of his game. As long as he could look down on her, she had someone to look up to. He liked that. Much to Lauren's credit, she *kept* the jeans and *dumped* her boyfriend.

If Lauren's story speaks to you personally, you are in a destructive relationship. A man who insists on molding you doesn't want a partner. Or an equal. He wants someone to control. I learned this lesson the hard way. You see, *I'm Lauren.* And this is *my* story.

I started dating Jason when I was seventeen. (I talk more about that relationship from a slightly different perspective in chapter 10, "It's Better to Be Lonely Out of a Relationship Than Lonely in a Relationship.") He was five years older than me, which definitely added to the allure. Young and impressionable, I was both in love and infatuated. But, sad to say, the relationship was lopsided. I wanted him to love me the way that I loved him. I think I kept waiting for that. Hoping. But, after a series of events similar to what I just recounted, I finally realized I was waiting for something that was never going to happen. Ever. And that was gut-wrenching—especially at nineteen, when my heart was so tender and vulnerable. When I had so much love to give. I was drowning in this pool of sadness and self-doubt. It was time. Ending the relationship was painful, but being *in* it was both painful and unhealthy.

In order to break away from a controlling partner, I had to choose *me.* I had to love myself more than I loved Jason. But here's the thing—self-esteem doesn't always precede action. Sometimes it's the action—making the better choice, the choice that screams "self-respect"—that is the catalyst for greater self-esteem. Choose *you*—and self-esteem will follow.

Hindsight is a great vantage point. But to get there—to achieve that level of clarity—we have to walk through the fear, the self-doubt, and the uncertainty in order to stand strong on the other side and claim the love and the life that we want. Only after moving on was I able to set a new standard. A *higher* standard. To be loved and to give love is one of the greatest gifts we can experience in life. Staying in the relationship with Jason would have meant disrespecting that gift. I wanted something better. And if anything in my story rings true in your life, then I want something better for *you* too.

In a healthy, caring relationship, a man loves you for who

you are. He values your thoughts, feelings, and opinions even if they're different from his. He acknowledges and appreciates what you bring to the table. And there's no need to control you, because he is secure enough with himself to want nothing less than an equal. He doesn't feel compelled to manipulate or guilt you into becoming something that you aren't or something that gives him a false sense of power and security.

True, when a man loves a woman, he wants her to be the best she can be. I get it. That was the argument Jason presented. But there's a difference between a man encouraging you to become everything *you* want to be and manipulating you into becoming everything *he* wants you to be. One comes from a position of strength and confidence. The other comes from a place of weakness and insecurity. A strong man can handle you growing into the woman you were meant to become. The other is afraid of losing you as a result.

ACTION STEPS:

- When one person says something, it's an opinion. When many concur, it's a consensus. If your parents and closest friends are pointing out the red flags in your relationship, pay attention. They see things that you may not. Assess the dynamics of your relationship to evaluate whether their concerns are valid.
- Ask yourself, *Do I like the person I am when I'm with him?* Depending on the nature of your relationship, this may tell you more than you *want* to know. But it will certainly tell you everything you *need* to know.
- Supercharge your confidence!
    - **Rewrite the narrative.** Shift the inner script from, "I'm not enough," to "I've learned. I've

grown. I know better now." You don't have to shrink, change, or earn his approval to be worthy. Don't give your power away!

- **Collect the evidence.** Start a running list of the things you've done that required courage, brains, or grit. Refer to it often, especially on days when self-doubt starts creeping in.
- **Choose people who choose you—as you are.** The right people won't need to mold you, fix you, or make you smaller to feel big.

SIX

OBSERVE HIS RELATIONSHIP WITH HIS MOTHER

Mom is a boy's first love. When he hit a home run, she was the one cheering him on. Her kisses healed everything from a scraped knee to a broken heart. And there was no problem that couldn't be solved over milk and cookies.

During his formative years, he developed ways of reacting to his mother's approval, love, compassion, disappointment, and criticism. Those responses carried over to adulthood. His pre-adult relationship with her set the stage for the way he now views women. Take note of how your romantic partner treats his mother. Observe their interactions. They reveal how he feels about women in general, and how he interprets his role in a relationship with them.

While I'm not a licensed therapist, I've noted a few unhealthy patterns to watch out for:

When a boy can do no wrong (or so his mother *thinks*), he may grow up believing he is the center of the universe, that *his* needs are more important than everyone else's. That the world owes *him*. After all, hasn't it always been that way? Since he could do no wrong, there wasn't anything for him to be held accountable for, right? So naturally, he grew up never having to own up to his actions, always blaming his negative outcomes on others.

Take John, for example. As a child and teen, his mom doted on him. It's true, mothers have a soft spot for their sons. I get it. I do too! This, however, was not a *soft* spot. It was a *blind* spot. John's inappropriate behavior never seemed all that inappropriate to her. And when his improprieties were too obvious to ignore, she simply blamed the whole situation on someone else.

Years later, when John was married to Chloe, he was selfish and unfaithful. He drank heavily—and frequently wet the bed—but insisted he didn't have a drinking problem. After Chloe filed for divorce, he told a friend, "She was impossible! I had to cheat! I had no choice." Seriously? I wonder where *that* lack of accountability came from.

When a mother is very overbearing and demanding, a teenage boy may acquiesce, developing little or no backbone or, feeling powerless, he may develop anger issues and overcompensate for his lack of control. Everyone is different, but this dynamic can play out by him trying to monitor and manipulate your every move. Not fun.

Men who grew up with **overly critical mothers** fear judgment and rejection. As a result, they often struggle with intimacy, vulnerability, and commitment. They also tend to experience women as being difficult to please. An internal soundtrack of "I can't do anything right" may replay on a continuous loop, often becoming a self-fulfilling prophecy and leaving them feeling inadequate and angry. Yet, other men with overly critical mothers develop a relentless drive to prove their worth. Until they address what's at the heart of the matter, they will feel like they're always striving *but never arriving*.

On the flip side, there are plenty of great guys out there, like Kyle, who had a close, healthy relationship with his mother. She adored him, yet she never wavered in her obligation as a parent—to help her son grow into a loving, responsible adult and to instill in him the confidence to make age-appropriate decisions. Though it wasn't always easy, and it certainly didn't win her any popularity contests, she was clear about what she expected from her son and had no qualms about calling him on the carpet when he crossed the line. There was a balance of love and discipline. It's no surprise that Kyle now enjoys an incredible relationship with his wife because his foundation for the way a woman should be treated was established long before he ever met her.

Unfortunately, not every man grew up with Mother of the Year. Does that mean he's doomed for failure, incapable of sustaining a healthy romantic partnership? Not at all. But it *does* mean he'll need to be very intentional about untangling his past. Like all of us, the more dysfunction he has experienced, the harder he will have to work on himself and his perceptions of women. Fortunately, therapy, seminars, workshops, podcasts, and books can help significantly, as long as he's willing to put in the work.

Of course, there are *many* factors that contribute to a boy becoming a man. But when a mother is loving, nurturing, and supportive—when she tempers that love with boundaries, discipline, and reasonable consequences—her son stands a much greater chance of growing up believing that women are amazing creatures who deserve love and respect. And wouldn't it be nice to be on the receiving end of *that!*

ACTION STEP:

- Think about the following questions: Does your romantic partner trust his mother? Does he respect her? Does he love her and feel loved by her? Did she hold him accountable for his actions? Was she nurturing? Did she help shape his values in a positive way? Obviously, the more "yes" responses, the better.

SEVEN

SOME MEN HAVE EMOTIONAL LIMITATIONS

When we see a five-foot-four teenager compete on a basketball court against his six-foot-three cronies, we might assume that slam dunking is not his forte. For that particular sport, he may have *physical* limitations.

When we observe a disabled child struggling to communicate with her peers, we smile and applaud her courageous efforts, knowing she is doing the very best she can. After all, she has *cognitive* limitations.

While we compassionately accept a person's physical and cognitive restrictions, we may not be as gracious when it comes to tolerating emotional limitations—especially in men—and more specifically, *our man*. Think about it, the emotional void isn't as outwardly apparent as its counterparts, so the expectations are different. We may also view his emotional capacity as being completely within his control—as simple as turning on the kitchen faucet full blast. Because of this, it's easy to make the absence of emotional availability mean something about us personally: *He's not that into me; I don't feel loved; I can't get him to open up.*

Although you want to feel connected, you'll save yourself a lot of frustration if you accept the fact that some men have emotional limitations—just like some men (and women) have physical and mental limitations. Don't take it personally. It's not about your level of lovability or worthiness. Don't let his emotional unavailability diminish your light!

It may be helpful to understand the shortfall. Here are a few reasons why emotional intimacy can be difficult for some:

- They may not feel safe exposing themselves.
- They don't know how to relate on that level simply because they've never learned.
- They grew up in an environment that wasn't emotionally nurturing.
- In their culture, it may be frowned upon, even harshly criticized, for a man to express emotion.

Whatever the reason, he had this "disability" before you came into the picture.

This doesn't mean he's a lost cause. First, try the Action Steps below to see if you can move the needle. If nothing changes, acknowledge that he has a "disability" and recognize that this is all he is capable of giving—without internalizing it. Without making it mean something about *you*. Don't spiral down to a place of self-doubt and insecurity. This is *his* limitation, *not yours*. Don't own it.

Next, determine if you want a relationship with someone who is emotionally unavailable. There is no universal right or wrong answer. It all depends on where emotional intimacy falls on your hierarchy of needs. For some of us, like me, emotional connection is important. For others, not so much. Keep in mind, we can also satisfy the need for connection with our girlfriends. What a blessing!

Finally, embrace—and act on—whatever decision you make. The right answer is the one that's right for *you*.

Remember, don't take his emotional limits personally. It would be tantamount to assuming a man who can't walk dislikes you because he didn't run over and give you a hug. Ridiculous, right? When we see someone in a wheelchair, there's no anger, no resentment, no self-esteem issues on our part. We simply accept their limits. Adopt the same objectivity with an emotionally unavailable man—or simply move on.

ACTION STEPS:

- While we can't change another person, we can shift the way we respond to, and interact with, them. Though the decision to make a change— any change—is their choice, create an environment where your partner feels safe and respected. Where he wants to transform himself and sees the benefit of doing so.
- If this strategy is working, even if it's only a minor improvement, acknowledge when he does open up and share his feelings. Help him to see the overall positive impact it's having on the relationship. What's recognized is repeated.
- Baby steps. If he has emotional limitations—if he's not opening up—either he doesn't know how, he has some serious trust issues, or he is scared to death of being vulnerable. *So don't judge his thoughts and feelings*. Be a good listener. There's a reason God gave us two ears and only one mouth.
- Let him talk. When he's finished, empathize and validate with statements like, *"I'm sorry you had to go through that." "That makes sense, given what you've been through." "That must have been so hard." "Look at everything you've overcome. You're strong and resilient."*

ALTHOUGH YOU LOVE THE LITTLE BOY IN HIM, MAKE SURE THERE'S A MAN IN THERE TOO!

I'm a pushover for little boys. There's something irresistible about that perfect combination of innocence and mischief in their boyish grins. I was reminded of it every day when my son, Michael, was growing up. I don't imagine he'll ever grow out of it; there's a little boy in *every* man. In fact, it's one of the many things that we love about them!

When I think back to my single days, the boyfriend who was the most fun, the most playful, the guy who could single-handedly transform a scowl into a smile with his crazy antics, could also take first place in "Least Likely to Grow Up. Ever." But I loved the kid in him. It was part of his charm. Unfortunately, he never quite made the transition to manhood. Decades later, he still sees himself as a victim in life, and parties like he did when he was twenty-four years old.

So how do you know if you're dating someone with Peter Pan syndrome, or just another cool, fun-loving guy? Consider this:

- **Does he refuse to accept responsibility for his actions?** Being responsible is a hallmark of maturity. If he's not there yet . . . I'm just sayin'.

- **Is every bad thing that has ever happened to him someone else's fault?** If he continually blames his parents, his boss, his friends (or you) for his circumstances, he's not looking at the one person who can turn it all around—himself. Besides, if he thinks other people control his misfortune then, by default, he must also believe they hold the key to his success and happiness. It's a disempowering and emotionally stunted mindset that will keep him from moving forward. If you have your act together, you'll soon outgrow him— if you haven't done so already.

- **Is he addicted to drugs or alcohol?** If this is the case, he has some issues to work through. Addiction is a disease. It's also a coping mechanism. He may be hiding from something, refusing to deal with reality, or lacking the life skills to handle his problems in a healthy and productive way. Whatever the case, he needs help overcoming his substance abuse. If you see yourself as the supportive girlfriend who will help him through this, then clearly, you have a big heart and a lot of compassion. Just remember, *he* has to be willing to take that first step.

- **Does he lie (and believe his own lies)?** The second life lesson most of us learned—right behind saying "please" and "thank you"—was, *never tell a lie.* If he still hasn't mastered the basics, I'd start to worry.

- **Does having a good time take center stage in his life?** We all like to have fun. I do. But if more important things like his education, work commitments, or promises he's made to you suffer as a result of his "toys" and "playtime," something is out of balance. Sure, you may have fun with the little boy in him, but it's the *man* you want to have a real conversation with. It's the *man* you want to respect and look up to. And it's the *man* you may eventually want to raise children with.

If you answered "yes" to several of these questions, maybe it's time to send him back to the sandlot with his juice box and LEGO set.

Little boys are adorable when they're seven years old, but do you really want one who is six feet, 200 pounds? Although you love the little boy in him, make sure there's a man in there too!

ACTION STEPS:

- If you want to have kids, do you picture the two of you raising children together? What about *teenagers*—a stage of life when a strong male role model is critical?
- Fast-forward your life five to ten years into the future. You'll likely be at a place where you've come into your own. Do you visualize him doing the same? Why or why not?
- If you see him progressing from a man-child to adult, distinguish if the storyline is coming from your head or your heart. In other words, are you projecting onto him all that you *hope* he'll become? Or has he given you evidence to support that expectation? Don't confuse time with growth. The years age us; they don't necessarily mature us.
- If you *don't* see him moving beyond man-child, what would be the benefit, *to you*, of staying with

him? And what would be the benefit, *to you*, of moving on?

- As you navigated these questions, what did you come to realize about him? About yourself? And about the viability of the relationship?

NINE

DATING A MARRIED MAN IS A NO-WIN SITUATION

You met the perfect guy. There's just one glitch—he's married.

Over time, you've convinced yourself that he's going to leave his wife. But, before you order monogrammed towels, let's put this in perspective. You *want* something that you *don't have*—top priority. And you *have* something you *don't want*—a man with no integrity. All the while, Mr. Douche Bag has the best of both worlds: the stability of a family and the excitement of the forbidden fruit. If you're looking for love and happiness (not to mention security, which, by the way, is off the table) chances are, you won't find it.

Dating a married man is a no-win situation. There's really no nice way of saying this, so here goes: It's morally wrong. And it seriously breaks the Girl Code. If the "other woman" knows he's married, she's a willing participant in a deceitful act that could break up a family. We're all familiar with the classic lines, "My wife doesn't understand me" and "The marriage was already over." So cliché. The marriage *wasn't* over. Not completely. It might have been in trouble, and the availability of another woman made getting some much-needed help and counseling a less desirable option.

Morals aside, let's see what's in it for the girlfriend. The wife (especially if there are children) usually gets weekends, holidays, and other special occasions. The Other Woman gets leftovers. His wife is by his side for the entire world to see; the relationship with his mistress must be kept a secret. He can't declare his love from the rooftop. And because *he* has much more to lose than *she* does, each date may be her last. Talk about a romance that tugs on your insecurities! That's a powerless place to be! Do you really want to settle for that?

Infidelity typically ends in one of two ways: Either he renews his commitment to his wife and kids or, less often, he leaves his family and marries the Other Woman. Whatever has kept him in the marriage this long—the kids, love, obligation, security, status, societal expectations, financial ramifications—is likely the same thing that will *continue* to keep him there.

But, for the sake of argument, let's say he chooses the girlfriend. If she were my best friend, or my little sister, here's what I would say to her: "Congratulations. You've won the battle but lost the war. Sure, he's yours now. But don't be so convinced that he's a prize worth keeping. Why would you want to build a life with a man who was so willing to throw his family away? A man who may start wandering again at the first sign of difficulty or boredom? You never know—the next family he throws away may be *yours*."

Maybe you know someone who ended up marrying the married man she dated. They may seem happy. But does the end justify the means? In my opinion, no. Affairs cause too much damage. They chip away at self-respect and self-esteem. People suffer. Children's lives are changed forever. And trust within the new marriage is questionable, at best. In the end, is it really worth it?

ACTION STEPS:

- If you're dating a married man, are you optimistic that he will eventually leave his wife and start a new life with *you?* Instead of musing about your days as the new Mrs., let's flip it and consider the other side as well. Take out a piece of paper and write at the top *Advantages and Disadvantages of Leaving This Relationship*. Draw a line down the middle. Think about the short-term *and* long-term pros and cons of ending it. Ink makes us think. So keep writing until there are twenty items listed, regardless of which side of the line they're on.
- Which column had the most "ink?"
- Take a look at the column *Disadvantages of Leaving This Relationship*. On a scale of one to ten, one being "when pigs fly" and ten being "tomorrow the sun will rise in the east and set in the west," what is the likelihood that each of those disadvantages will improve over time?
- What did you notice? Has your perspective shifted? Call or text a friend or accountability partner to discuss.
- If you're dating someone who's married, don't you want more than that? If so, then behave like you're *worth* more than that.

TEN

IT'S BETTER TO BE LONELY OUT OF A RELATIONSHIP THAN LONELY IN A RELATIONSHIP

When I was nineteen years old, my mom said something to me that changed my life.

I was two years into my relationship with Jason. Sexy. Charming. *And older.* He was twenty-four. I didn't see it at the time, but it was an unhealthy relationship. He used put-downs to control me. Unkind, disrespectful remarks like, "I need a woman, not a little girl," left me feeling insecure and "not enough." (Ironically, for someone who "needed a woman," he had a pattern of pursuing younger girls.) *Hmm. Interesting.*

For months, I seriously considered breaking up with him. I knew he wasn't good for me, but my mind and my heart were battling it out and, unfortunately, my heart was in the lead. Ending it would have been a no-brainer if he was a jerk all the time. But there were some great moments. Things about him that I really loved. Deep conversations that were engaging and sparked my curiosity. He was charismatic and I was in awe of his ability to inspire and motivate his work team. It was a destructive relationship, but he gave me just enough to keep me holding on, just like "The Challenge" that you'll read about in chapter 13.

My mother could see my unhappiness and sense my

uncertainty. One day, she said, "Lisa, it's better to be lonely *out* of a relationship than lonely *in* a relationship. When you're lonely *out* of a relationship, it eventually gets better. But when you're lonely *in* a relationship, it only gets worse."

Wow! That was one of the best insights anyone has ever shared with me. Thanks, Mom! The "jeans" incident in chapter 5 came on the heels of this advice. I broke up with Jason and that pivotal decision started influencing my choices and, by extension, the woman I was becoming.

My mom was right. When we stay in an unhealthy relationship it gets worse because we sink deeper into emotional quicksand, and we're not capable of bringing ourselves up for air. Each day, we lose another piece of who we are. It's no wonder we start seeing ourselves through someone else's distorted eyes. The emotional abuse convinces us that this is what we deserve. So we stay put and the cycle continues.

On the other hand, when we terminate a bad relationship, loneliness diminishes over time, and we eventually heal. We start to reinvent ourselves. We begin to gain perspective, dignity, confidence, and self-acceptance. We reclaim our power. The downtime allows us to reevaluate ourselves and our relationship goals. Only then are we in a position to attract a healthier relationship because we believe we truly deserve it, and we're making fresh decisions based on a whole new set of rules—rules that include self-respect, boundaries, and a positive view of ourselves.

Be courageous! *You Got This!*

ACTION STEPS:

- Ask yourself, if I end the relationship now, how will I feel about my decision a month from now? A year from now? Five years from now? After hypothetically distancing yourself, what did you notice? Were there any patterns as you mentally visited each point in time? What were your key takeaways after doing this exercise?

- Focus on improving yourself. Create an ongoing list of books you'd like to read, hobbies that spark your interest, and a passion you would like to pursue or rekindle.
  - Identify two things from the list that you're going to start with. Take the first step *today*.
  - Continue with your list and revise, as needed.
- For a fun variation of this, play goal-setting bingo. Make or purchase a blank bingo card, filling in each square with a goal that you would like to achieve over the next twelve months. Yes, you can fly solo, but to supercharge your commitment while building and supporting your "village," I say enjoy the journey with a friend or two (or three!). For every friend you are playing bingo with, keep a blank square open for them to write a goal that they have for *you,* and vice versa. You don't have to play blackout bingo, where you X out every goal on the card (although you could). Start small and build: Go for five in a row vertically, horizontally, or diagonally. Each time someone in the group gets a bingo, get together and celebrate each other's successes. Then, at the end of the year, meet up and talk about the journey. Incorporate a variety of goals and have fun with it! Here are a few goals from my current goal-setting bingo card:
  - Take dance lessons
  - Eat at a Michelin-starred restaurant
  - Exercise five out of seven days a week, for an hour
  - Make gnocchi from scratch
  - Publish *You Got This!*

- Go to a speakeasy
- Lose ten pounds
- Create five new clients
- Plan a themed dinner party
- Read something uplifting each day
- Visit a city I've never been to

Looking forward keeps us from looking back and significantly minimizes the post-relationship blues.

ELEVEN

YOU DON'T JUST MARRY A PERSON, YOU MARRY A LIFESTYLE

Today I met the man I'm going to marry. Whether you've heard those words in a movie, declared them yourself, or listened as your BFF gushed on and on about "the one," that single sentence conjures up thoughts of Happily Ever After. And why not? With Ariel and Cinderella as role models, how could we expect anything less? If only it were that simple!

It's not.

We don't just marry a *person*. We marry a *lifestyle*. More specifically, we marry an economic status, a communication style, and a set of core values and beliefs. As you'll hear me say throughout the book: It's better to be proactive on the front end than reactive on the back end. So as we consider these three lifestyle factors, think about your "absolutes" and "desirables"; your deal-breakers versus your nice-to-haves.

You Marry a Financial Lifestyle

According to Dr. John Gottman, world-renowned for his work on marital stability and divorce prediction, "Money is one of the most common sources of conflict for couples." So let's take a look at what may happen if there's financial disparity between what you want and what actually is.

Let's say you're in love with an amazing man—who happens to have limited earning potential. I'm not suggesting that material comforts are more important than love. I am, however, encouraging you to think about what really matters most to *you*. For example, do you want to be a stay-at-home mom while your children are young? If so, will his earning potential afford you that opportunity? Will you feel bitter if it doesn't?

Gender roles have shifted in recent years. In 40 percent of US families with children under eighteen, the mother earns at least half of the household income. And 16 percent of married couples report that the woman earns more than her spouse. This changing tide works for many couples. And for some, it just doesn't. On both sides of the equation, many factors come into play, including upbringing, cultural norms, education, religious beliefs, and media influences, to name a few. If you were to earn more than your husband and, in your mind, work a lot harder, would you be filled with a sense of pride . . . or resentment?

You Marry a Communication Style

It's not uncommon for there to be an introvert and an extravert in a romantic relationship. In general, there's usually an attraction between contrasting personality types; they tend to balance each other out. Here's the caveat: If the gap between two communication styles is as wide as the Grand Canyon, you're going to run into issues—both as individuals and as a couple—within your personal and professional circles.

Marlee found this to be true after dating Chase for almost a year. In actuality, it was true the entire time, but she needed time to admit it to herself. Some background: Marlee was articulate, conversational, and held her own in both new and familiar social settings. Though Chase had other good qualities, he felt awkward in social situations. In fact, it was agonizing for him to be with people he did not know well. So, he avoided situations where he was expected to interact. Given the imbalance, their relationship was going to head in one of three directions: Marlee would have to make her world—and herself—smaller, Chase would need to get comfortable being uncomfortable, or they would go their separate ways, realizing that this was not a good lifestyle match.

Their communication styles were so polarized, I knew if Chase wasn't willing to overcome his fears, Marlee would soon outgrow him. Knowing I couldn't push too hard or Marlee would dig in her heels, I said, "You know, Marlee, there are going to be communication differences in every relationship. You'll have to decide whether it's a good balance with you and Chase, or if it's too extreme. You'll figure it out."

Several months later, she did.

Marlee had invited Chase to an important family function. There would be a few familiar faces and many that he would be meeting for the first time. After making excuse after excuse, he eventually acquiesced, only to be a no-show the day of the event. Knowing this was not a communication lifestyle Marlee wanted to marry, she ended the relationship.

You Marry a Set of Core Values

Before you tie the knot, understand each other's core values and how they line up. If you're a starry-eyed romantic who believes that love conquers all (I get it. I used to be one), you may wholeheartedly believe that love will give you the power to overcome anything. You're close. Love may give you the *desire* to bridge the gap, but it won't give you the *belief system* to reconcile significant, value-based differences. You need to be on the same page with the big stuff: the values that have the potential to bring the greatest joy—or drive the largest wedge.

For example, let's say you're very family oriented. Do you visualize weekly Sunday dinners with all the relatives gathered around the table à la *My Big Fat Greek Wedding*? Does he? Are you able to meet somewhere in the middle?

Or maybe your husband-to-be is expected to relocate every couple of years, while feeling rooted in your community gives you a much-needed sense of belonging. Is there a workable compromise?

Or what if your fiancé has a different faith? Some couples have been able to successfully navigate the terrain of religious dissonance. But what happens when you're both quite devout and your religious traditions and routines conflict? Or when your opposing faiths present some lifestyle differences? If you have children, should they be taught Mommy's religion? Daddy's religion? Neither? Both?

Think about your priorities and expectations. The bigger the variance between the life you envision and the one you wake up to each day, the more frustration you *both* will experience. *You,* because although you love your husband, you may not love the life you've built—or have failed to build— together. *Your husband,* because on some level—consciously or subconsciously—he'll internalize, and possibly feel responsible for, your dissatisfaction. A good man wants to please you, and a good woman wants to please her man. But if either senses that they can't, they're either going to feel bad about themselves, bad about their partner, or find someone they *can* please. Once negative feelings persist and escalate, one or both partners will become dispassionate, indifferent, and emotionally detached.

You don't just marry a person. You marry a lifestyle. Knowledge is power. So before you say, "I do," ask, "Do I?" *Do I really want to marry this lifestyle?* Think about how you envision the next forty or fifty years—not simply from a financial standpoint but from a communications and value-based perspective. Know your deal-breakers. They're different for each of us. Discuss. Negotiate. Compromise. Most of all, know yourself.

ACTION STEPS:

- Get real. For each of the questions above, write out your responses. Again, there are no right or wrong answers. Just the right answers for *you*.
- At the beginning of this chapter, I asked you to consider your deal-breakers and your nice-to-haves. We looked at three lifestyle areas: financial, communication, and values. If you could only align on two out of the three, which would you choose? Why so?
- As you were going through this exercise, what did you discover about yourself and your relationship priorities?

TWELVE

ARE YOU IN LOVE WITH THE IDEA OF BEING IN LOVE?

I could always tell when Lola was seeing someone new. It wasn't simply because she was watching *The Notebook* for the umpteenth time. Or that her singing lingered long after her morning shower. Rather, the dawn of a new romance always coincided (practically down to the minute) with the phasing out of another guy—someone who, a few short months ago, she was equally crazy about. Lola suffered from a condition that, if left untreated, could render her single for the rest of her days. First, let me say, "til death do us part" may not be your end game. It may not even appeal to you in the least. And that's fine. Marriage isn't for everyone. But if you would like to share your life with someone special, and the idea of family and growing old together appeals to you, keep reading.

Lola was in love with the *idea* of being in love. A Love Junkie awaiting her next fix.

True, there's nothing that quite compares to the euphoria of falling in love. No wonder Lola wanted to do it over and over again! Unfortunately, sometimes we're not really in love. We're simply addicted to the excitement, romance, and absence of predictability that come with a brand-new relationship. You may be thinking, *Sounds good to me, Lisa. What's the problem?*

Well, initially, there is no problem. We go through the heart-racing, starry-eyed stretch of the romance (so far, so good), but that stage doesn't last forever—even in the best of relationships—because we can't sustain that level of physical and emotional fervor indefinitely. As soon as her heart rate slows down and her breathing stabilizes, the Love Junkie becomes bored, anxious to recreate—with someone new—that exhilaration all over again. (This, by the way, is the female counterpart of the "Sprinter" in chapter 2.) If this cycle is never broken, the Love Junkie could drift from relationship to relationship, reliving the pinch-me-I-must-be-dreaming phase, but never going beyond that to something more meaningful and lasting. More importantly, she will never discover what's holding her back from being "all in"—a barrier that will likely resurface in other areas of her life.

Fast-forward: Lola is now married to a man who is the gold standard for a good catch—someone for whom mothers lift an eyebrow and give a side glance as they whisper to their daughters, "Now *that's* the kind of man you want to hold out for."

Lola never would have gotten to this enviable place in life if she hadn't ventured beyond being in love with the idea of being in love. She attributes the pivot to having greater self-awareness, realizing and appreciating what she *does* have, and letting her walls down. All of this enabled her to be more open to deeper relationships.

Being in love is what it is. But the *idea* of being in love is whatever we want it to be, limited only by our imagination. That's what makes it so compelling. It's pretty cool when we can dream up every delicious detail. But let's be honest. It's not real. And when we knowingly, or even unknowingly, avoid reality, there's an underlying reason why. It could be a commitment issue, a fear of abandonment, an aversion to boredom, a holding out for the **BBD** (Bigger Better Deal), or a dissatisfaction with who we are or where we're at in life. At any rate, it's an exit strategy that allows us to get our feet wet without venturing off into deeper, riskier—and more fulfilling —waters.

If, like Lola, your revolving door is getting more foot traffic than Macy's on Black Friday, it's safe to say you are likely in love with the *idea* of being in love.

ACTION STEPS:

- If you're in love with the idea of falling in love, spend some time each week falling in love with *you*. It doesn't matter where you go or what you do as long as it's a solo journey, it inspires joy, and it allows for self-reflection.
- Ask yourself, *With the onset of each relationship, am I moving toward something or avoiding something?* Gravitating toward something is usually rooted in growth and self-awareness. Avoiding something— when it's driven by fear rather than boundaries— often signals unfinished business. If it's the latter, what are you afraid of? And what would you have to come face-to-face with if you broke the Love Junkie habit?
- Write down your thoughts. What is something new that you discovered about yourself?

THIRTEEN

A "CHALLENGE" IS SOMETIMES JUST ANOTHER WORD FOR AGGRAVATION

SWWMFC (Smart Woman Who Makes Foolish Choices) looking for MWKHTKAGG (Man Who Knows How to Keep a Girl Guessing). Must be willing to flirt with other women in front of girlfriend. Ideal candidate will have diffi- culty opening up. Must be commitment-phobic.

Although I've never actually seen that profile in an online dating site, there are certainly women who can't resist the allure of a man who's hard to get. After all, we love a chal- lenge, don't we, girls? Well, here's a news flash: A "challenge" is sometimes just another word for "aggravation."

So why would a "smart woman" sell herself short? For the same reason Las Vegas casinos will never go out of business: People love the *expectation* of a payoff almost as much as the payoff itself. Just like our gambling counterpart, we're waiting for the big reward—the prize that makes the preceding losses (or near wins) all worthwhile. The more time invested, the greater the seduction, because we *know* our patience is about to pay off. At the tables, the chips appear and vanish—*as do his sincere gestures*—convincing us we're just one play away from hitting the jackpot. He gives us just enough positive reinforcement to keep us in the game, as we eagerly anticipate the next romantic payoff. Attentive one minute and aloof the next, he keeps us coming back for more.

In my late teens and early twenties, I passed up some great guys while wasting precious years on men who offered little more than a challenge in return. Jay was one of those guys. He had difficulty making a commitment. *That's because he's picky*, I told myself. I labeled his lack of communication *introspective*. And when it came to flirting with other women, I reasoned, *He's just being friendly. Besides, I'm above all that jealousy stuff.*

Clearly, my narrative was distorted.

Fortunately, I've learned a thing or two since then, like why this type is so appealing:

1. **Mystery:** We are drawn in by the intrigue of a good mystery. We want to figure him out and unlock the secrets of his heart. But since he never commits or opens up completely, our job is never done. And therein lies the trap.

2. **He's hard to get:** When we acquire something (*or someone*) too easily, we tend to question its worth. The flip side is also true. The more difficult the win, the greater the perceived value. That notion holds true with scholarships, job promotions, and the purchase of a brand-new car. Not men. It took me years to learn to appreciate a good man. I hope you'll shave some time off that. You'll keep some of the good ones from slipping away.

3. **Ego**: *If I can turn him around. If I can be the woman he finally falls in love with, well, then, that sort of says something about me, doesn't it?* Maybe yes. Maybe no. But that type of validation is not healthy because you're evaluating your worth through *his* eyes instead of your own. Your ego is a lousy substitute

for your brain. If you want to boost your self-esteem, there are healthier and more productive ways to accomplish that.

4. **Adrenaline rush:** His lack of predictability, combined with the emotional highs and lows, can be exciting. Just remember, the higher you soar, the harder you fall.

If the opening paragraph sounds like your significant other, it's time for a new love interest. So how do you break free from "The Challenge?" The same way you stop *any* addiction. You quit. You make a decision to walk away. Simple as that. I did it, and so can you.

You Got This! Should it really be *that* much work to keep him interested? Seriously, who needs the "aggravation?"

ACTION STEPS

- Find a "sponsor"—bestie, parent, sister, trusted colleague—someone who has your best interests at heart. It's time for rehab. You need a "detox" that puts you on the road to confidence recovery, peace of mind, self-acceptance, and mental clarity. You're not flushing out drugs and alcohol. But you're purging something just as harmful: toxins from an unhealthy relationship that have left you doubting yourself. Are you ready to take your power back?

- Okay then. After breaking up, absolutely no contact with him for the next ninety days. You heard me. Ninety days. That means no texts. No phone calls. No looking at his Instagram stories. In fact, block him for those ninety days. No accidentally-on-purpose running into him. That also means not *responding* to his texts and phone calls. And, by the way, texting him to tell him not to text you *is contact*. Be strong. This won't be easy. When a person is going through rehab for drug or alcohol addiction, the detox stage is unpleasant. But it's an inherent part of recovery. This is no different. As you're eliminating the addictive relationship, it's going to be painful at first. At the very least, it will be an adjustment. This is part of the process. "I'm tapping out," won't work here. You've got to work *through it.*

- As you're purging, start replenishing. Every day, do something—multiple somethings—that lift your spirits. Here are some ideas: performing a random act of kindness; getting together with a good friend; reading a faith-based passage or something else uplifting, like a book you've been excited to pick up; taking a walk on a gorgeous day; watching a movie that makes you laugh so hard you feel like you've just done a killer round of abs in an advanced Pilates class; trying a yummy new food or restaurant; sitting on a park bench watching four-year-olds play; or whatever it is that puts you in a positive frame of mind, keeps you in the moment, and reminds you that the greatest joys can come from the simple things in life.

- I talk about goals in several places throughout this book, offering a different framework each time. It's worth repeating because setting and achieving goals strengthens our confidence and resilience, promotes self-acceptance, and fosters a positive mindset. Set a thirty-day, sixty-day, and ninety-day goal. This is about *you* and reconnecting with what lights you up, independent of a love interest. It will

keep you reaching forward, rather than looking
back.

- Write down the three things you like most about
  yourself. (I know, this may feel a little goofy.) Ask
  three people who care about you to do the same.
  Read the accolades. Every day. Chances are "The
  Challenge" made you question your worth: *What's
  wrong with me? Why doesn't he love me enough to commit?*
  The recognition will remind you of who you are
  when you're at your best!

FOURTEEN

BEHAVIOR REPEATS ITSELF

My mother was instinctively wise when it came to human behavior. She had this Spidey sense about her that was impressive, but sometimes unnerving—especially when she was right. And particularly when she was right about guys I was dating. *I hated when that happened!* She could see the naked truth in someone long before there was even a blip on my radar. I remember her saying, "Lisa, one of the best ways to determine how a man is going to treat you years from now is to notice how he treats other people." I wish I would have done more listening and less eye-rolling. Her simple yet profound advice could have put therapists out of business!

It's true, if a guy generally relates to his family, colleagues, buddies—and even strangers—with respect and dignity, chances are he will do the same with you. Yet all too often when we see a man being dishonest, disloyal, or rude to someone else, we mistakenly—and naively—conclude, *he would never do that to me.*

Case in point: A married man pursues you. He's everything you've ever wanted—smart, attentive, incredible chemistry, lots of personality, gets along with your friends and family, is financially stable, and makes you laugh; he's warm, kind, and understanding. *Yeah, to everyone but his wife!* Don't flatter yourself into thinking he's cheating because you're irresistible. You may be a catch, but he's cheating because he's a cheat. Given the right circumstances, he may do the same thing to you. And even if he doesn't, just the mere *possibility* of betrayal will always be in the back of your mind. What kind of relationship can you expect to have when the absence of trust and respect are what brought you together in the first place?

Consider another hypothetical: Let's say your romantic partner has a hair-trigger temper. You've witnessed his road rage. You've heard his screaming reach glass-rattling decibels. You've seen the fist imprints in the walls of his apartment. Would it be realistic to assume that he would never "lose it" with *you*?

Not all bad behaviors are as extreme as cheating or uncontrolled anger but are just as important to concede. For example, does he have the potential to disregard your feelings? Has there been evidence of this in his other relationships?

Here's a reality check: Behavior—good or bad—repeats itself. While many of us accept this truism, we may believe that when it comes to being the recipient of a man's bad behavior, *we* are the exception to the rule. *But this is different. I'm different.*

The thing you have to remember is that his behavior is about *him. It's not about you.* Let me say that again so it really sticks. His behavior is about *him. It's not about you.* To look at this objectively, you have to take yourself out of the equation and recognize that his actions are a reflection of his character. And his character—anyone's character, for that matter—was established long before you came along. Because of that, it only makes sense that his bad behavior will repeat itself. Like an old pair of shoes, we get cozy with the habits we've been "wearing" for a long time. Good or bad, right or wrong, people typically return to what's "comfortable."

The way your love interest treats other people is a valid barometer for how he will eventually treat you—once the novelty of the relationship wears off. So if you're dating someone who is amazing to everyone he knows, you can probably count on him being equally amazing, if not more, to you. On the other hand, if he shows signs of being selfish, disloyal, insensitive, easily triggered, or non-communicative toward others, either get out . . . *or consider it a sneak preview of things to come.*

When people show you who they are, believe them.
—Maya Angelou

ACTION STEPS:

- Write down one negative behavior you've seen in him. Not something small, like the way he squeezes the toothpaste. I'm talking about a potential deal-breaker or a major character flaw.
  - What is your emotional reaction to this behavior? For instance: *When he acts this way, I feel angry/jealous/sad/embarrassed.*
  - What excuses, if any, are you making for him? Would you make those same excuses for someone you weren't romantically involved with? Write down your thoughts. It will help you process not only *what* you're doing but *why* you're doing it.
  - Repeat, if needed, with additional negative behaviors.
  - What are your epiphanies?

- Now, write down three positive behaviors that you've seen in him.
- What is your emotional reaction to these behaviors? For example, *When he acts this way, I feel loved/appreciated/calm/joyful.*
- Does he *consistently* demonstrate these positive behaviors?
- What does all of this say about his character?

FIFTEEN

TWO WRONGS
DON'T MAKE A RIGHT

Many of us grew up with the classic Mommyism, *Two wrongs don't make a right.* Let's see how the idiom holds up to a relationship gone bad.

Dylan and Stefanie had been together since her senior year in high school. They had a very rocky relationship, but Stefanie loved him, and she really wanted it to work. The longer she stuck it out, the harder it was to break away because she had already invested so much time in the relationship. The way she saw it, the bumpy road ahead was shorter than the one already traveled. At about the eight-year mark, Stefanie was at a crossroads. She wanted to get married, but Dylan wasn't ready to commit.

Really? After eight years, if the guy doesn't know, he knows! Stefanie was vacillating between breaking up with Dylan and waiting it out in the hopes that he would declare his undying and eternal love for her.

Our conversation went something like this:

Stefanie: "Lisa, do you know how old I'll be five years from now if I don't stick it out and I have to start all over again with someone new?"

Me: "Um, the same age you'll be five years from now if

you *do* stick it out—only with a broken heart, some wrinkles that you had to work way too hard for, and 1,826 days that you'll never get back." (Okay, I didn't actually calculate the math—including the leap year—right there on the spot, but you get the point.)

Stefanie: "But I've invested all this time training him; getting him to the point that he is now. After all my hard work, am I just supposed to step aside and let another woman reap the benefits?"

Me: "Only if you want to keep your sanity. Your dignity. Your life. Besides, Stef, if he were that much of a prize—if his "training" actually produced some good results—your frustrations would have ended a long time ago. Think of it this way: He gets to be someone else's headache now. Count. Your. Blessings."

Don't marry the wrong person simply because you've put years into a relationship. Two wrongs don't make a right. The time you've spent in a less-than-desirable relationship (wrong #1) doesn't justify putting *more* energy into it (wrong #2).

The average female lifespan in the United States is 81.1 years. We want to accomplish and experience as much as we can in those eight decades, so we get it in our heads that the clock is ticking and we have to achieve particular milestones by a certain age. Complete our education. Tick tock. Land the ideal job. Tick tock. Marry the perfect guy. Tick tock. Buy our dream house. Tick tock. Start a family. Tick tock . . .

Despite our best intentions, life has its own timetable. And love—at least the right kind of love—doesn't always show up when we want it to. So let's remember our mother's words of wisdom: *Two wrongs don't make a right.*

Regardless of your age, have a little *faith* that the right one is still out there. Have the *confidence* that you deserve him. Have the *patience* never to settle, and you'll experience more smiles than tears and more memories than regrets.

ACTION STEPS:

- We can feel stuck in the present when we can't clearly see the future. The fastest and healthiest way out of this rut is to set a personal goal. Make it a short-term goal. Three to six months. Short-term goals are easier to focus on, and quite honestly, if your relationship has become stagnant, or the wrong guy has taken a toll on your self-esteem, you'll want to see results sooner rather than later. This will not only build your confidence but it will also expand your world and help you see what's possible for *you*—independent of a romantic partner. As you become bigger—in the best possible way—the people in your life who are disrespecting you, or simply don't appreciate you, become smaller. At that point, it's much easier to distinguish who is contributing to your life, and who is diminishing it. That's an empowering perspective!
- Track your progress.
- As you work toward your objective, ask, *In what ways has my outlook on the relationship changed? How has my perspective of myself shifted? What did I discover? And how will these insights help me to be a better version of myself?*

SIXTEEN

MAKE A RESERVATION FOR FOUR

I once worked with a woman who shared a brilliant strategy with me. Before she accepted a bona fide job offer from a male employer, she suggested that they, along with their spouses, go out to dinner. It wasn't cocktails and fine cuisine she was interested in. It was information. Her theory was that her boss-to-be likely treated his female colleagues—and particularly his female direct reports—the way he treated his wife. By the end of the evening, she knew if they were a team. She could tell if he respected women, welcomed their ideas, and valued—even encouraged—their input. She could also sense if he was chauvinistic and if he had the "little woman" mentality. Unbeknownst to the man sitting across the table, the dinner was her way of extracting attitudinal and behavioral information about the person she might be spending eight to ten hours a day with. Provided that everything else about the job measured up, this was the final frontier. By the time dessert and coffee were served, she knew if he would be an advocate or an adversary. More importantly, she knew if she would be accepting or declining the position.

I thought her game plan was fabulous. So much so that I knew it had a broader application. If you're dating someone who has definite marriage potential, make a reservation for four—the two of you and his parents. Watch the dynamics between his mother and father. You'll be amazed by how much insight one meal can provide.

Does your boyfriend's father address his wife respectfully? Does he welcome her opinions? Is he somewhat amused, if not charmed, by her idiosyncrasies? Or is he easily annoyed? Does he belittle her? Dismiss her thoughts as unimportant? Even allow her to speak? Their verbal and nonverbal communication will provide the answers you're looking for.

So why all the junior detective work? Well, when you and I were growing up, in many ways we learned what we lived. What we were familiar with became our comfort zone. We began to imitate, sometimes unintentionally, our parents' interactions. A son is far more likely to treat women lovingly when he has witnessed his father genuinely cherishing his mother. Of course, there are exceptions. But unless we've done a significant amount of personal development and have a high level of self-awareness, we—as imperfect humans—tend to revisit the behaviors that we're comfortable with, not necessarily the behaviors that will serve us well.

Make a reservation for four. Make lots of them. Dinners. Family outings. Afternoon lattes. Watch. Listen. And learn. Because the apple, as they say, doesn't fall too far from the tree.

ACTION STEPS:

- During dinner, here are a few conversation starters that have the potential to evoke some emotion and reveal the nature of your boyfriend's parents' relationship.
  - *How did you meet and fall in love?*

- *They say if you live with someone long enough you start to become like them. Is that true? Have you taken on each other's personality traits?*
- *What's your secret to staying happily married all these years?*

- Listen to *what's* being said, *how* it's being said, as well as what is *not* being said.
- Ninety-three percent of communication is nonverbal. Eye contact, touch, facial expressions, and voice inflection all speak louder than the actual words being spoken. That considered, what are your overall impressions?
- If there are any red flags, don't jump to the immediate conclusion that your romance is doomed. Some of us have learned our best relationship lessons by having an example of what *wasn't* working in our parents' marriage and then intentionally making the necessary adjustments. If your warning bells were going off during dinner, have a follow-up conversation and get your partner's take on what happened. His perspective on the issue is just as relevant as the issue itself.
  - An open-ended question like *What did you think when your dad said such-and-such?* will highlight his attitude on something you may have found offensive.
  - Or, if your partner had a clear nonverbal reaction to something in the conversation, you can later make the observation, *Babe, I noticed the expression on your face when your dad did such-and-such.* Your partner's response will offer insight into his attitude and values.

SEVENTEEN

WHEN "FOREVER" IS IN THE JOB DESCRIPTION, PICK A WINNER

Imagine you are an executive recruiter working with Fortune 500 companies. Your reputation and livelihood depend on your ability to consistently search out, pitch, and recommend top performers for key positions. You're good at your job. You're thorough. And you leave nothing to chance.

Let's say your biggest client calls you on Monday morning and gives you a unique assignment: Recruit a CEO. This person will ultimately be responsible for the success of the company. His or her leadership style is critical. In fact, it will either catapult the company on a trajectory of success or cause its demise. You and your client spend the next three hours on strategy—setting clear objectives and crafting a candidate profile. Your client concludes the meeting with something you've never heard before: "Oh, and by the way, I know it's a bit unconventional, and I'll explain more later, but this is a *lifetime position,* so find us a winner."

What? A lifetime position?

A heavy responsibility rests on your shoulders. You can't fail; too much is on the line. Your client is counting on you. Your client's entire team is counting on you. Of course, being the conscientious recruiter that you are, you carefully review the job description, qualifications, and company culture. You fine-tune the candidate profile. Your ideal prospect is top tier. You won't find this gem just anywhere. They will keep good company.

What was that catchphrase our grandmothers were always spouting? *Birds of a feather flock together?*

While this prospective CEO is unknown to you at the moment, chances are someone in your network—someone you trust—already knows them. You'll start there. And since history repeats itself, you'll look for an established record of success. Once you develop a shortlist of high-potential candidates, you'll want to note how each prospective CEO resolves conflict and overcomes challenges. To keep perspective, you'll do a thorough background check. Finally, you'll recommend that your client observes how the top candidates interact with key members of the team. This is, after all, a lifetime position.

Your job and the success of the company hang in the balance, so the regret-resistant steps that you'll take are all quite reasonable; in fact, they're astute, right? But now, substitute the word "life" for job and "family" for company: Your *life* and the success of the *family* hang in the balance. Yep. The stakes are even higher!

When it comes to marriage, are we as judicious as the conscientious "executive recruiter?" While Hollywood, and society at large, encourage us to "follow your heart," when we're thinking long-term we also have to follow our head and our gut.

Unfortunately, Katie "hired" a life partner without putting nearly enough thought into the "job description," completely ignoring his track record as well as his lack of character. After five years of marriage, she filed for divorce. Admittedly, Katie did not put the time and forethought into one of the most important decisions she would ever make. Logic and common sense flew out the window. She was in love (and in lust), and she felt amazing when she was with Tim. But the way we *feel* when we are with a man should not be the extent of the "screening" process.

If you're dating and think this guy is "the one," or would at least like him to be, consider what's at stake for yourself and your future children and pick a winner!

ACTION STEPS:

- I am not a fan of resume dating—you know, dating someone just because they look great on paper and check all the boxes. It leaves no room for chemistry or instincts. That being said, and I know this sounds counterintuitive, I think it's a good idea to write a "husband profile," just like our fictitious executive recruiter wrote a candidate profile. It will help you think through what's most important to you when the relationship is a "lifetime position" as opposed to a fleeting romance. And, as you articulate what you want in a life partner, you'll notice that you'll begin visualizing this person and this relationship. You'll even start feeling the positive emotions that come with having that person in your life. It's the Law of Attraction and it comes down to these three components: Be clear on what you want, visualize it, and feel the feeling of having it *now*.

- A well-thought-out question can expose a person's character. I know this isn't the most romantic of inquiries but ask anyway. If you've been dating a while, hopefully you've already had a few deep conversations. So try this one: *What's the biggest mistake you've made in life, and what did you learn from it?* His response will tell you if he's humble, accountable, and someone who learns from the past. It takes two to tango, as the saying goes. So if he blames everything on his previous partner, his former boss, or his no-longer-my-best-friend, he either has a very big ego . . . or a very big blind spot.

EIGHTEEN

LOVE IS LIKE BEING IN A BOXING RING

Love is like being in a boxing ring. We can spend every round protecting ourselves and, sure, we'll never get hurt, but at some point we have to open up and engage if we want to get in the game.

Life lesson: We can't guard our heart and leave it open at the same time. A protected heart doesn't discriminate. It doesn't know how. So it blocks *everything*—the disappointment, the humiliation, the pain, the betrayal, as well as the sheer joy and happiness that come with falling head over heels in love and sharing our life with someone special. In short, a door that's locked swings in *neither* direction.

Granted, once our heart has been pulverized, the knee-jerk reaction is to protect it. It's easier. Safer. Our guard goes up, insecurities take over, and survival instincts shift into high gear. Instead of being ourselves and allowing all that's lovable to shine, we block it. We hold back. We're stingy with our feelings. And we project bad motives onto our partner. Here's the irony: We're afraid of being hurt and alone, so instead of playing full-throttle, we sabotage a good thing and, in the end *we feel hurt and alone.*

Falling in love, and nurturing love, require vulnerability and courage. The two are inextricably intertwined. Brené Brown, author and research professor, put it best in her book *Rising Strong* when she said, "Vulnerability is not winning or losing; it's having the courage to show up and be seen when we have no control over the outcome. Vulnerability is not weakness; it's our greatest measure of courage."

It's worth noting that courage is *not* the absence of fear. Courage is walking through the fear because we're committed to the person, ideal, opportunity, or belief waiting on the other side. Courage means moving forward, in spite of fear.

The stronger we become on the inside, the more courage we can express on the outside. Continue to grow and evolve. If he leaves you, mistreats you, disappoints you, or deceives you, you will survive! Whatever has gotten you this far in life —grit, determination, a positive attitude, or downright stubbornness—will again see you through if the relationship doesn't work out. Be someone who will love wholeheartedly and still be complete if it doesn't go the distance. *You Got This!*

If the fear of being "injured" outweighs the courage to "take the prize," it will be nearly impossible to sustain a healthy relationship. If we're unwilling to be vulnerable, we will never know what could have been. Regret comes not only from doing the things we wish we hadn't but from *not* doing the things we wish we had.

ACTION STEPS:

- Close your eyes. Retrace what happened the last time a romantic partner hurt you. Replay the scene with as much visual, emotional, and auditory detail as possible. It's hard. I know. Stay with me. Allow the feelings to come to the surface. As you relive this moment in time, write down the top three emotions that came up for you.

- Now, as you continue to reflect, rather than focusing on how *your partner* screwed up (he slept with your best friend; he lost your engagement ring in a poker game; he was emotionally abusive, etc.), think back to the warning signs you either missed, or ignored. For example, he looked at other women like they were ice cream and he was the spoon; he had an addictive personality; he had a habit of being condescending to waiters and other people in the service industry; and so on.

- As you visualize your past in the rearview mirror, let's imagine that you have a do-over. What actions do you see yourself taking as the warning signs come into focus? How can you be more astute and assertive? Be aware of what you would say and do differently. As you mentally rewrite the script, act out the scene either in your head or, if possible, out loud. Recalling and reliving what he did to hurt you will keep you locked in victim mode and prevent you from "getting back in the ring." On the other hand, revisiting the *warning signs* puts you in control of your own life again. You'll find that it will give you perspective and insight into *his* character instead of an unfair interpretation of the entire male species.

- How does it feel to have taken control of your life? Internalize those feelings. This cognitive restructuring promotes neuroplasticity (the brain's ability to adapt and change) and builds new neural pathways in the brain. Hold on to that power. It's yours. Write down the top three emotions you are experiencing *now*. How do they compare with the emotions you were experiencing at the beginning of this exercise?

- Rather than assuming every man is going to break your heart, disrupt the pattern and get back in the ring!

PART TWO

RESPECT YOURSELF

SETTING BOUNDARIES

KINDRED SPIRITS

NINETEEN

IDENTIFY YOUR ROCKS

Have you ever noticed how some people are able to make choices with ease and confidence while others agonize over which road to take, even with relatively simple decisions?

There's a widely circulated story about a college professor who recognized this shortcoming and came up with a clever way to illustrate it. Over the years, his analogy has been shared so often that it has practically become part of modern wisdom.

As the story goes, he stood at the front of the classroom with a few simple items laid out on the table. When the lecture began, he picked up a large empty jar and filled it with several big rocks—each a couple of inches wide. He asked his students if the jar was full, and naturally, they said, "Yes."

Then he reached for a container of small pebbles and poured them in. After he gently shook the jar, the pebbles settled into the open spaces between the rocks. Again, he checked with the class. Again, they believed the jar had reached its capacity.

But he wasn't finished. He took a box of sand and let it

pour into the jar until it filled every last gap, leaving no space at all.

Only then did he explain the point. The jar represents your life. The rocks symbolize what's most important—your health, your closest relationships, the people and priorities that give your life meaning. If everything else fell away, your life would still be full.

The pebbles stand for the other things that matter—your job, your home, your responsibilities. They're not your foundation, but they add to your life.

And the sand? That's everything else. The distractions. The trivial details. The things that feel urgent but aren't actually important.

If you fill your jar with sand first, you won't have room for the pebbles or the rocks. And if you spend your time and energy on the small stuff, you'll crowd out the things that truly deserve your attention.

The message was simple but powerful: Your life will always feel full—it's just a matter of what you choose to fill it with. Know what your "rocks" are.

The difference between decision-makers and decision-fretters is often a matter of having a hierarchy of priorities—a mental or written list of who and what are most important. This will help you base your decisions on what you value most in life while reminding you to spend time on what's important rather than filling up the hours with "sand." When faced with a difficult decision, you will already have a structure in place to help you evaluate your choices and determine the best path to take.

Such was the case with Carly. In her mid-twenties, she was on a fast track to success . . . and a nervous breakdown! She had quickly earned the respect of colleagues and upper management. The company loved her, but there was a price to pay. She was stressed out, had no personal life, despised her boss, and had gained fifty pounds in one year's time. Contrary to the advice of friends and family to "stick it out, at least until the next promotion," Carly turned in her letter of resignation.

If you were in Carly's shoes, that may or may not have been the best choice for *you,* but the decision was the right one for *Carly* because her health and mental well-being were her "rocks." She didn't get distracted by the money or lured by the next rung on the corporate ladder. Although this was a *difficult* decision for Carly, it wasn't a *confusing* one because she had a hierarchy of priorities that allowed her to respect herself, be objective, and cut to the heart of what she valued most in life.

Setting value-based priorities will help you determine whether or not you should attend a certain college or university, move into a new home, start a family, accept a lucrative employment offer, marry a particular person, change careers, be a stay-at-home mom, accept a job promotion, or leave the town you grew up in.

Decisions become easier once you set value-based priorities. Take care of the "rocks" first—the things that *really* matter. The rest is just "sand."

ACTION STEPS:

- When it comes to prioritizing your life, the "right" answer is the one that works for *you.* To help determine what that is, write down your top five core values—the people, things, or principles that are most important to you. Your faith? Your family? Honesty and integrity? Your home? Your car? Professional achievements? Loyalty? Creativity? Leaving a lasting legacy? Love and connection? Whatever those top five values are, write them down. Then force rank them from one to five. This is your compass. It points to true north. You will always feel "off" when your actions and choices don't reflect your core values. This exercise can especially help when fear of missing out (FOMO) has you feeling pulled in ten different directions. It's so easy to say "yes" to every invite, every opportunity, every shiny thing that pops up. But here's the truth: FOMO can trick you into chasing things that look good on the outside but don't actually line up with who you are and what you want. But don't overthink it either. Getting stuck in analysis paralysis will only leave you drained and second-guessing yourself. Sometimes the real stress comes not from the wrong decision, but from making no decision at all.

- According to Tony Robbins, bestselling author and world-renowned coach, all humans are driven by six core needs—universal motivations that influence almost everything we do. Here's my take on them.
  - **Certainty:** We all crave a sense of stability—the comfort of knowing we're safe, secure, and able to avoid unnecessary chaos or pain. It's the part of us that wants to feel grounded and in control.
  - **Variety (Uncertainty):** At the same time, we also need change. We seek out new experiences, surprises, and a little unpredictability to keep life interesting. Too much routine can leave us restless or bored.
  - **Love and Connection:** Humans are wired for closeness. Whether it's through deep friendships, romantic relationships, or a sense of community, we long to feel understood, accepted, and emotionally connected.
  - **Significance:** We want to matter. To feel seen, valued, and recognized for who we are.

This need fuels our desire to stand out, to be appreciated, and to believe our presence makes a difference.

- **Growth:** We feel most alive when we're evolving—learning, stretching, and becoming more of who we're meant to be. It's the drive to improve, to level up, and to keep moving forward.
- **Contribution:** There's a deep fulfillment that comes from giving back. When we know we've helped someone, supported a cause, or made life a little better for someone else, it gives us purpose.

- To one degree or another, we each possess all these needs. Choose the two that are most dominant. Then, when making decisions, after first determining what choice best aligns with your core values, ask yourself how the decision holds up to your top two human needs. What—if anything—might you need to adjust so these two needs are being met?
- If you find yourself torn between two options, try the "coin flip test," a strategy that has been popularized by therapists, coaches, and writers. Here's how it works: Assign one option to heads and one to tails. The insight comes not from what the coin says, but from your gut reaction. Are you relieved or disappointed? That emotional response reveals what you *actually* want.

TWENTY

OPEN A PERSONAL WELLNESS ACCOUNT (PWA)

I t's 8:00 p.m. You'd give anything for a bubble bath and a glass of wine. *But first, the bills.* As you scroll through your online account, you realize that you're overdrawn. Yikes! Note to self: *Make a deposit. Now.*

Banking 101: **Withdrawals must not exceed deposits.** Common sense and ethical standards—not to mention the threat of being turned over to the district attorney's office—keep this regulation in check. If only there were a system in place that helped us monitor withdrawals on a *personal* level.

Women are born nurturers, and multitasking is in our DNA. So it's easy for us to become physically, mentally, and emotionally "overdrawn." Think about the people and organizations you've devoted yourself to just in this past month—friends, parents, romantic partner, congregation, coworkers, boss, clients, children, siblings, community, and favorite charities. They've been the recipients of your wholehearted generosity. Unfortunately, our minds and bodies don't have an automatic shutdown feature that kicks in when we've depleted our internal resources. That requires a manual reset. We do that by taking care of ourselves.

Starting today, open a Personal Wellness Account (PWA). Each day, make deposits by doing three things that feed your mind, your heart, or your body—wellness rituals that lift your spirits, nourish your creativity, or indulge your senses.

The alternative would be to continue making withdrawals until you feel exhausted and resentful or are completely tapped out with nothing left to give. A lack of self-care will eventually take a toll on your health, attitude, and disposition. In an ironic twist, your relationships—the very ones you're trying to enrich and preserve—will suffer in the end. Keep in mind, it's not about the amount of time you spend. It's about consistency and being fully present in the moment without obsessing over what's next on your to-do list.

If you're feeling some resistance to starting a Personal Wellness routine, you're not alone. When my coaching clients face this hurdle, their challenges typically fall into one or more of the following categories: time, the need for significance, or guilt. Let's take a look at each. Then, at the end of the chapter, I'll offer some recommendations to help you overcome those obstacles.

Time: Why is it that we have time to be frustrated, angry, and unclear (all of which slow us down), but we don't have time to do things that help us feel centered, joyful, and focused (which, by the way, contribute to our productivity)? Being proactive on the front end reduces the need to be reactive on the back end.

The need for significance: When we find ourselves being all things to all people, there's a tremendous sense of importance that comes with the territory. It feels good to be needed. To be the "go-to girl." There's nothing wrong with the need for significance, but when it comes at the cost of depleting us, it's time to make an adjustment.

Guilt: If you think a PWA is selfish, or simply unnecessary, reconsider its financial counterpart: *Banking withdrawals must not exceed deposits.* To give it more context, do you feel guilty when you deposit $2,000 in your checking account? No. It feels good! It feels responsible. There's a sense of security and peace of mind knowing that the money is there if and when you need it. The same holds true for a PWA. But, if you're not quite convinced, let me state the obvious: A beautiful garden needs water, sunshine, and good soil, or the plants and flowers will wither away and die. And think about what would happen to your car if you didn't put oil in the engine. It would break down. Try driving across the country on half a tank of gas. Your *car* can't run on empty. What makes you think *you* can? You need to put "gas" in y*our* "engine" if you want to keep running.

The deficiencies mentioned above are obvious, signaling to us that it's time to give our bank account, our garden, our car, what they need. But mental and emotional bankruptcy are gradual. Not as easy to detect. There are no watchdogs. No one pressing charges for non-sufficient wellness (NSW).

You can only offer others what you already have to give. Make daily deposits into your PWA. It may not pay the bills, but it will give you a fresh perspective and the mindset necessary to *be your best* and *give your best*.

ACTION STEPS:

- When opening a PWA, if **time** is your challenge:
  - You may have to re-proportion your schedule. We all have twenty-four hours in a day, seven days in a week. If you find yourself continually starring in the movie called *There Just Aren't Enough Hours in the Day*, I get it! See chapter 22, "Saying 'Yes' to One Thing Ultimately Means Saying 'No' to Something Else."
  - Block out Personal Wellness time on your calendar. Once you decide that window is off-

limits to everyone and everything else, you'll be amazed at how other commitments and requests seem to naturally flow around that.

- ○ Color code your calendar using the following applicable categories and any others you would like to add: spouse/significant other, family, friends, worship, work, household responsibilities, school, volunteer/charitable work, hobbies, and personal wellness. This approach will help you identify, evaluate, and reassess how you're spending your time. It will also help hold you accountable for making three Personal Wellness deposits each day. As you'll see from the list below, some of those ideas only take a couple of minutes, while others are more involved and time-consuming. Delete and add to the list to make it your own.
- ○ Be consistent. Start small and build. You may not be able to take a two-hour hike, but can you schedule time for a twenty-minute walk? Make it easy. If it feels like the time commitment is too much, you'll be tempted to quit before you even get started.
- When opening a PWA, if the desire for **significance** is your challenge, ask yourself: Is my feeling valuable and needed worth more than my health, well-being, and longevity?
  - ○ In what *other ways* can I feel important, special, relevant, and significant?
  - ○ Is my feeling valuable and needed worth more than my health, well-being, and longevity?
- When opening a PWA, if **guilt** is your challenge:
  - ○ You are likely "shoulding" yourself to death. *I **should** be cleaning the house. I **should** have finished my proposal by now. I **should** be studying for*

*finals. I **should** be spending more time with my kids.* Let's reframe those "should" statements in a way that removes the guilt, keeps your commitments intact, and restores some balance to your life.

- Instead of *I should be cleaning the house,* try this on: *Twenty years from now, who's going to care that my house looked perfect? It's not a museum. I want it to look nice, but also feel lived in. I'll tidy up, then go to Pilates.*
- Rather than *I should have finished my proposal by now,* here's an alternative: *After I go for a run, I'll be more clearheaded, and I'll power out that proposal in no time at all.*
- If you find yourself saying *I should be studying for finals,* take out the "should," acknowledge the importance of your education, and ask yourself a question that will help you strike a balance. For example, *Doing well in this class is important to me. What's one thing I can do right now to recharge my battery so that I get a good grade in the class, but not burn out in the process?*
- And now for the granddaddy of all guilt-inducing "shoulds"—parenting. More specifically, motherhood. As a mom with two "kids" in their twenties, I have to say, there's no area in my life where I have second-guessed myself more. For all you moms out there, a big part of our identity is connected to motherhood. We wholeheartedly want to do it so well; so perfectly. Try not to "should" all over yourself. With the example above, *I should be spending more time with my kids,* consider this

> way of reframing it: *I love spending time with my kids. And when I also do something for myself, I'm teaching them boundaries and respect—for me and themselves. They are the most important people to me in the world. But it wouldn't be fair to my kids if I let them grow up thinking the entire world revolves around them. It also isn't fair to them if I become so depleted and frustrated that I easily lose patience with them and I'm not present when I am with them.*

- Here are some Personal Wellness deposits that I've suggested to my clients, or have incorporated into my own routine:
  - Take a walk surrounded by nature or something that inspires you.
  - Keep a gratitude journal and write down two things you're thankful for from that day.
  - Sit on a park bench with a good book or sit and watch children laugh and play.
  - Get a facial.
  - Get a massage.
  - If it's been one of those days, get a facial *and* a massage.
  - Have lunch with your bestie. Busy day? FaceTime them instead. Share a funny story or remind each other why you're BFFs.
  - Put on a great piece of music and dance like no one is watching.
  - Enjoy the sunset.
  - Create a vision board.
  - Sit down for fifteen minutes with a coloring book and a big box of sharpened Crayola crayons.
  - Join, or start, a book club.

- Watch a movie that makes you laugh so hard, you have to cross your legs and hope for the best.
- Do Amy Cuddy's two-minute power pose. (You may have to look up Amy's TED talk.)
- Take a candlelight bubble bath with lavender essential oil.
- Go to a museum and make up a story in your head about the artist, the subject, or the scene.
- Take up a new hobby.
- Sit on the beach.
- Sign up for a fun class at the local community college.
- Read an inspirational passage, quote, or poem.
- Go to the gym.
- Take a Pilates class.
- Pour yourself a glass of wine and pair it with your favorite cheese or chocolate.
- Review your goals. Visualize them. And feel the feeling of having achieved them!
- Curl up with a good book, even if it's just for fifteen minutes.
- And my favorite. Buy a pretty card. Write yourself a nice note inside. Put it in the envelope, stamp it, and mail it to yourself. When it's delivered and you read it a couple of days later, I hope you'll smile and remind yourself that it's moments like this—the snippets of time you take to invest in yourself—that inspire and empower you to continue to create powerful moments for *others!*

TWENTY-ONE

SURROUND YOURSELF
WITH POSITIVE INFLUENCES

You're relaxing in front of the television, watching a movie, when a pizza ad comes on. I'm not sure where they find mozzarella that stretches to infinity, but my chicken parmesan would love to know! After watching bite after mouthwatering bite, you make a beeline for the refrigerator in search of something scrumptious—as if a tasty treat miraculously appeared since the last commercial break. Nope. Nothing new. So you open your Doordash app and order a pizza. *With extra cheese.*

Whether or not you consciously connected the dots between cause and effect, you *were* influenced by the commercial. That's exactly what advertising executives are counting on. So are their clients. In fact, according to industry reports, companies spend around $300 billion a year on advertising. And that's just in the United States alone! They know that a well-crafted ad stimulates our senses, engages our emotions, and creates a compelling narrative to buy. Executives are "betting the bank" that their strategies will yield a strong return on investment. And why not? What we see, hear, and experience all affect our thinking, our desires, our moods, our decisions, and our actions. And while advertisers can manipulate everything from culinary cravings to the car we fantasize about driving, commercial influence pales in comparison to the impact of social media *and* the people whose company we choose to keep. Think about it: If a thirty-second pizza ad got you off your comfy couch, bolting toward the kitchen, doesn't it stand to reason that you're being influenced—for better or for worse—by the people around you?

This insight has been consistent throughout the ages. Consider what ancient wisdom *and* contemporary thought leaders have said about the correlation between who we are and the people around us:

"Tell me who your friends are and I'll tell you who you are."
  —Spanish proverb

"Do not be misled. Bad associations spoil useful habits."
  —1 Corinthians 15:33 (NWT)

"The one walking with the wise will become wise, but the one who has dealings with the stupid will fare badly."
    Proverbs 13:20 (NWT)

"The more you surround yourself with positive messages, positive images, and positive people, the better life gets."
  —Michele McKeag Larsen, founder of The Joy Team, in an interview with *The Huffington Post*

"The people you surround yourself with will determine the level of your success."
  —John Maxwell, author, speaker, and leadership expert

"Surround yourself with the dreamers and the doers, the believers and the thinkers, but most of all, surround yourself

with those who see the greatness within you, even when you don't see it yourself."
—Attributed to various sources

"The quality of a person's life is most often a direct reflection of the expectations of their peer group."
—Tony Robbins, author, coach, motivational speaker

"Choose people who lift you up."
—Former First Lady, Michelle Obama

While most of us can identify the positive people in our lives, sometimes it can be a little trickier to spot the negative influences because the ill effects can creep up on us, especially with overexposure. In other words, we can become desensitized to the "Pessimistic Petes" and the "Debbie Downers." Personally and professionally, here are ten identifying marks that I've observed in positive and negative people. While no one fits neatly into one category 100 percent of the time, start noticing where the people in your life fall on this continuum. And by the way, this is a great gut check to *personally* revisit from time to time.

A positive person asks, "How can I bring this idea to life?" A negative person concludes, "Um . . . this can't be done." A positive person learns and grows from adversity. A negative person uses adversity as a catchall excuse for their addictions, poor behavior, or inability to achieve their goals. A positive person—regardless of circumstances—counts their blessings. A negative person scratches their head and wonders, *What blessings?* A positive person infuses you with energy. A negative person sucks the life out of you. A positive person asks, "How can I help?" A negative person often thinks, *No one helped me. Why should I help you?* A positive person rolls with the punches. A negative person feels like throwing a few punches. A positive person recognizes the good in others—including you. A negative person sees the flaws in others—including you. A positive person believes in you and cheers you on. A negative person can't wholeheartedly believe in you because they don't wholeheartedly believe in themselves. A positive person sees challenges as steppingstones. A negative person sees challenges as roadblocks. A positive person believes life happens *for* you. A negative person believes life happens *to* you.

We are all influenced by the world around us—by what we read, what we listen to, what we watch, what we talk about, what we see on social media, and what we choose to think about. Most of all, we are affected by the people we surround ourselves with. Our close associates influence us mentally, emotionally, and energetically. They have a strong effect on our attitude, character, decisions, and future. Choose wisely. If you're going to let someone live in your head, rent-free, lease the space to a worthy tenant!

ACTION STEPS:

- Be intentional about the company you keep. Immediately after an interaction with someone, be attuned to your energy level, what you're thinking about, and how you feel.
- Take a close look at the podcast, website, and social media content you follow. What's the focus? For instance, if you frequent motherhood sites, do the creators concentrate heavily on venting about how their kids aren't sleeping, the mess they make, and how hard it is overall? Or do they acknowledge that it's tough while providing suggestions on how to have smoother mornings, keep tidier homes, and streamline meal prep? If you follow personal finance content, do the sites primarily focus on how high the interest rates are

and how much more difficult it is for young people to buy a home compared to their parents or grandparents? Or, instead, do they take a more proactive stance and help you budget, minimize debt, and appreciate the benefits of making small contributions to a retirement fund?

- Make one positive shift in each of the following areas:
  - What I'm reading.
  - What I'm listening to.
  - The conversations I engage in, whether in person, virtually, electronically, or through social media.
  - The internal monologue, or negative thoughts, in my head. To challenge negative thought patterns, please see the Action Steps in chapter 45, "The Celebration Plate."
  - Finally, and most importantly, the people I surround myself with.
- A couple of considerations on this "positive shift" Action Step: First, it's important to note that when we're making changes for the better, sometimes it requires *adding* something to our routine and at other times we're *eliminating* what is no longer working for us. Second, you can either make these shifts all at once, or you can address them one at a time. Obviously, the faster you surround yourself with positive influences, the more quickly you'll experience the benefits. The important thing, however, is that the changes are sustainable. So find a pace that works for you.
- Ask yourself, *What do I most want to be remembered for? And who are the people in my life who align with, and support, that vision?*

- If you want to be a positive influence on others, recognize that you can only give what you already have. Your output cannot exceed your input. It would be like trying to power a Tesla with a phone charger.

SAYING "YES" TO ONE THING ULTIMATELY MEANS SAYING "NO" TO SOMETHING ELSE

Have you ever said "yes" to a request and immediately wished for a rewind? Maybe you acquiesced when you really wanted to say, *Are you kidding me?* If so, keep reading.

We all have twenty-four hours in a day, seven days in a week. Yes, I'm stating the obvious. But here's what might not be so apparent: When we say "yes" to one thing, we are, by default, saying "no" to something—or someone—else. And more often than not, that "someone else" is you or the people you care about most.

For many, that three-letter word is on autopilot. So let's take a look at *why* we say yes, the benefits of saying no, and how to determine what is yes-worthy. Then we'll explore ways to navigate the "no" conversation more gracefully, confidently, and assertively.

Why We Say Yes

When we say yes, it's usually for one of the following reasons:

- We don't want to hurt their feelings.
- It's an opportunity to try something new.

- It gives us a sense of importance and significance.
- We like being seen as the go-to girl.
- We want to look good.
- We'll be perceived as valuable.
- We want to help out a friend.
- Job security.
- We're people-pleasers. We like being liked and well thought of.
- FOMO.
- We hate letting someone else down.
- It's an opportunity to expand our skill set.
- If we say yes, next time they'll owe us one.
- Saying yes will positively impact our future.
- We're all about making a profound difference.
- Saying yes will contribute to the happiness and well-being of others.

The Benefits of Saying No

- Too many yeses can leave us feeling overwhelmed and resentful. The irony is, when we begrudgingly say yes, we can find ourselves getting upset and frustrated with the *other* person. Wait a minute! Have we forgotten that we actually had a choice in the matter? These negative emotions are misdirected. *We* are the person we're upset with and we're projecting annoyance onto the person who made the request. We may even find ourselves muttering under our breath, "I can't believe they had the nerve to ask me to do that." Actually, *they* have a right to ask. And *you* have a right to respond authentically to it. We always have a choice. There may be an unpleasant outcome. But we always have a choice. And the minute we think we don't, *that's* when we give our power away.

- "No" allows us to leverage our time and focus on what's most important—close friends and family. Our health. Our goals. Projects we've been wanting to take on (or complete). Giving back to the community. Experiences that bring us joy and allow us to inspire joy in others. Whatever your "most important" happens to be.
- Saying no, when appropriate, eliminates the negative energy that often accompanies a disgruntled yes.
- Are repeated types of requests coming from the same person because of their poor planning, or lack of responsibility? If so, that should be a hard pass. And a conversation. "No" puts the accountability and ownership on them to either get their act together or come up with an alternative option or resource. In situations like this, "no" has the potential to be a huge growth opportunity for you. And for them.
- Standing up for ourselves and finding our voice leaves us feeling more self-assured. So, saying no can actually ignite our confidence and courage.

Am I advocating an absolute "no" under all circumstances? Absolutely not!

Decide What Is Yes-Worthy

To determine what is yes-worthy, set your internal GPS. The destination: your core values. The best route: decisions and responses that support those core values. When there is a direct connection between our values and how we spend our time, our lives have purpose. We get the sense that we're moving toward something meaningful, as opposed to being incredibly busy but getting absolutely nowhere.

When time and values are *not* aligned, we feel unsettled, unfulfilled, and tired. Let your responses—whether yes or no—reflect your core values. This will look different for each of us, so I won't give an exhaustive list of what is yes-worthy and what isn't. Once you're absolutely clear on your core values, it becomes easier to set goals and priorities, make decisions, and reply with a yes or a no. Set that internal GPS!

ACTION STEPS:

- If you already have a "full plate," stop asking for seconds!
- Whether it's work-related, a personal favor, or a social invitation, whenever possible, let the requester know you'll get back to them within twenty-four hours.
  - First, that will prevent the knee-jerk "yes" response.
  - Second, it's going to give you the space to evaluate the pros and cons of taking this on.
  - And third, you'll have the chance to untangle why "yes" might have previously been your go-to response. You'll start seeing patterns. Your reasons for saying—or wanting to say—yes are likely going to stack up in one or more of the categories above. Once you understand *why* you say yes, you're in a much better position to ask yourself, *Do my frequent yeses truly serve me, the people I love, my goals, and my core values?*
- In chapter 19, "Identify Your Rocks," I asked you to determine the five values that are most important in your life. Let's revisit those.

- With those values in mind, decide if the ask is yes-worthy.
- If it's a no, use the suggestions outlined below.

Finding Your Voice: How to Say "No" in a Constructive Way

1. I've said this before, but it's worth repeating: It's easier and less frustrating (for everyone!) when we're proactive on the front end instead of being reactive on the back end. Set yourself up for success long before a potential "no" conversation. Let people know your boundaries and you will get fewer unreasonable and time-consuming requests. It will be easier to find your voice and have a positive, constructive conversation if you've already set the expectation. This is particularly helpful for the introverts out there who need white space in their calendars, but who sometimes feel pressured to accept a social invitation. If friends, family, and colleagues are already aware that you don't like to crowd your calendar and typically do only one social thing on a three-day weekend, you can often decline without offending them.

2. Be genuine in your communication. Although you'll want to give thought to what you'll say and how you'll say it, if you sound too rehearsed, you'll come across as inauthentic.

3. Validate. Acknowledge that this is important to them.

4. Be respectful. Treating the other person with kindness and dignity will build bridges instead of walls, even in the face of turning down their request.

5. Be confident in your tone and body language. This lets them know you are grounded in your decision. If they smell fear or hesitation, it's game over.

6. Whenever possible—and this is important—offer a viable alternative or solution that will create a win-win. If it's a work request, this approach positions you as a problem-solver. A critical thinker. Someone who thinks outside the box. If it's a personal ask, this lets the other person know you actually do care about something that's important to them. On both fronts, it helps mitigate disappointment.

TWENTY-THREE

INVISIBLE BOUNDARIES ARE WORSE THAN NO BOUNDARIES AT ALL

I was watching a group of kids play soccer when some commotion broke out.

"Out of bounds!"

"Was not!"

"Was too!"

"Where's the line?"

"Dude, there is no line."

"Then how do you know it was out?"

Exactly. Those kids set "invisible boundaries"—limitations that are not clearly defined.

Grown-ups do the same thing *off the field*. We create these rules, these expectations, that we want other people to comply with but then completely fail to communicate those limits. These boundaries are "invisible" *to everyone except the one who created them*.

Here's an example of how an invisible boundary led to ambiguity, misunderstanding, and the demise of a business relationship. Michelle, an interior designer, had hired Candace as a subcontractor. When Candace submitted her invoice, Michelle didn't want to pay her for all the hours she had billed since Michelle had to repair something Candace had broken and should have either replaced or fixed on her own time. That's a completely reasonable expectation. The problem was, this was an invisible boundary—a policy that existed only in Michelle's mind. She never expressed it to Candace, either verbally or in writing, before *or* after the fact. In the end, Michelle ate the costs. She was seriously annoyed at both herself and Candace. In fact, she never hired or referred anyone to Candace again. As with most invisible boundaries, there's never a winner.

Invisible boundaries are worse than no boundaries at all because we (mentally and emotionally, never literally) hold others to a standard they aren't even aware of. Then, when they cross the line, we get angry, frustrated, and yes, very resentful. From *their* perspective, they don't have a clue what all the drama is about, and we end up with the same chaos I saw on the soccer field that day.

Before we can set reasonable—and visible—boundaries, let's look at why we often don't impose them, and how we can overcome that challenge:

1. **Fear of loss:** *If I express what I want, my boss, family, friend, significant other, or whoever, may decide I'm not worth the trouble.* We have to first decide that we *are* worth the "trouble." Once we embrace that mindset, and truly believe it, others will also. On the flip side, if we don't respect ourselves enough to acknowledge our own value and set limits reflective of that, others will likely develop a negative perception of us.

2. **Fear of what others think:** *Um, I don't want to appear demanding.* Guess what? People value boundaries. Limits seem to shout, *Hey, I respect myself, so you should respect me too.* If people know up

front what the rules and expectations are, then they have a choice—they can participate or not. When people have a say in the matter, how is that demanding?

3. **Fear of confrontation:** *I don't want to get into a disagreement.* I get it. But there's more confrontation and "drama-fication" when people don't know our expectations up front. In chapter 27, "Confrontation Doesn't Have to Be Confrontational," I'll take you through a six-step process that will help you confidently navigate difficult conversations.

Setting boundaries is simply a matter of expressing what we want in a clear, non-aggressive, friendly manner, then holding ourselves and others to that standard. A confident attitude is key. If we're wishy-washy or uncertain in what we want, the other person will perceive our boundary as an *option*. Whenever possible, help the other person to see how this is a benefit to *them*. And keep the lines of communication open by respecting and acknowledging the other person.

Let's say you're planning your wedding and you and your fiancé have established a budget. You've barely recovered from sticker shock after interviewing the florist when your mom and dad hand you a list of eighty of their closest friends that they would like you to invite. At $200 a head, you do the math and suddenly wish your parents weren't so popular. Here's how you could approach the situation, using the acronym BE CLEAR, from the Action Steps below:

Mom and Dad, I love that you've always been so enthusiastic about the milestones in my life (acknowledgment and **respect**). *I love your friends. Some of them I've known since I was a little girl. As much as I would like to have them all at my wedding, I can't.* (Be **confident**. Stand tall. Shoulders back.) *It would put us thousands of dollars over budget* (**explain** your "why") *and it wouldn't be smart to* *start out my marriage with that type of financial stress.* (A **benefit** to them: You're their daughter and they want what's best for you.) *How about if we go over the list together and pick out the 30 people you'd most like to have at the wedding.* (Set **limits**. Hold them **accountable** to the boundary.) Defining the **expectation** early is always best. Once again, it's easier and more effective to be proactive on the front end than it is to be reactive on the back end. When all parties understand the boundaries from the outset, there is a greater chance that clear and respectful communication will follow.

It isn't always easy, and depending on the circumstances, there may be some give and take before a clear boundary is set.

Whether we're interviewing for a new job, involved in a romantic relationship, or maintaining healthy friendships, let's make our boundaries visible. Once the lines have been clearly drawn, we'll avoid needless aggravation and misunderstandings.

ACTION STEPS:

- Brainstorm areas in your life where you need to set clear boundaries. If nothing immediately comes to mind, ask yourself where you're experiencing resentment. We often feel this emotion when a line has been crossed that we either haven't expressed or held the other person accountable to.
- Set visible boundaries, using the acronym BE CLEAR.
    - B—Communicate how the boundary is a **benefit** to them.
    - E—**Explain** your "why."
    - C—Be **confident.**
    - L—Verbalize your **limits.**

- o E—Set clear **expectations.**
- o A—Hold yourself and others **accountable.**
- o R—Be **respectful** in the way you communicate.

TWENTY-FOUR

BE COMMITTED,
BUT NOT ATTACHED

It was almost 10:00 p.m. when I received the call that it was happening again. "Come over *now!*" I implored her. "You're spending the night at my house." Within fifteen minutes, my friend Paige was in my living room, slowly and painfully recounting every detail of the argument, the evidence of his abuse beginning to take shape above her left cheekbone. I was enraged! *How could he do this to her? And how could she let this happen again?*

True to form, I was doling out advice faster than a Vegas blackjack dealer could divvy up a deck of cards. *It's a good thing she has me here.*

The next morning Paige left my house full of uncertainty. She had "a lot of thinking to do." *Really? He hit her—more than once. He was a jerk. A bully. A coward. She was young. There were no children in the picture to consider. Seriously, what was there to think about?* From my vantage point, the decision seemed obvious: Leave him, press charges, and see how *he* holds up to the abuse *behind bars*! In hindsight, I do realize this is easier said than done. Relationships are complicated.

In the weeks that followed, I obsessed about Paige's marriage and her impending decision. *Is she okay? What if he hits her again? She has to get out of that house for good!* I spent weeks worrying about her while she seemed to be going on with her life, unencumbered by the situation at hand. And then it occurred to me. I was more wrapped up in her problem than she was. I later had to ask myself, *why?* What was this triggering in me?

As it turned out, she reconciled with her husband. There were flowers. Tears. Makeup sex. He swore he'd never touch her again. She loved him and wanted it to work. She *believed* it could work. I was emotionally exhausted and the only thing I wanted in return was for Paige to have a shot at happiness. Selfish as it sounds—because it really wasn't about me—I felt like my angst and sleepless nights were in vain.

Paige's ordeal was a turning point for me. Since then, I've learned to *be committed, but not attached.* I realized that it didn't make sense for me to be more emotionally invested in people's lives than they were.

The Oxford English Dictionary defines the word committed as "dedicated or devoted to a cause, ideology, activity, or person," and the word attached as "joined or connected physically." With this in mind, let me explain what I mean by *be committed, but not attached.* When we're committed to someone, we create the space to be wholeheartedly loyal and supportive from *any* distance. But when we are attached, we are tethered to their issues and their emotions. Where they go, we go. And when their issue is resolved, and especially if they've chosen a path different from what we would have chosen, it's a lot to untangle! We're better equipped to help someone out of quicksand when we're hoisting them out from dry land as opposed to being in the thick of it, joined at the hips. When we are committed, but not attached, we're doing everything we can to help and support the person we love but it's not taking an unhealthy toll on us—and *our* happiness is not dependent on *their* happiness.

Admittedly, there are times when I struggle with this

because it requires a balance of compassion and boundaries—
two things I value greatly that can sometimes pull me in two
different directions.

But I'm far more aware of that pull now. So whether the
women I care about are dealing with an abusive relationship,
a cheating boyfriend, a toxic friendship, a dysfunctional work
situation, or anything else that calls for both honesty and a
listening ear, I'm still there—to cheer them on, to support and
encourage them, to listen with my eyes, ears, and heart, and to
share a box of Kleenex and a pint of Häagen-Dazs.

But I no longer give more thought to my friends' problems
than they do.

I'm there for them. But I'm only willing to help them to
the extent that they're willing to help themselves. That
doesn't mean they have to arrive at the same decision I
would have if I were in their shoes. But in the end, they
have to care about making a positive change in their *own*
lives, because if they don't, all my compassion, all my
advice, and all my sleepless nights won't make a difference
anyway.

ACTION STEPS:

- Take a moment to think about, or write down,
  your response to the following question: What is
  my primary payoff when I give someone else's
  situation more thought than they do? For example,
  is it a heightened sense of importance? The
  satisfaction of being needed? Does it make me feel
  more connected to them? Here's a big one: Is it
  keeping me from facing something in my own life?
  Did I, or someone close to me, go through a
  similar circumstance and now I'm projecting a lot
  of emotion onto this situation? For me, coming to

Paige's rescue satisfied an unhealthy superhero complex.

- Now that you have identified the payoff, consider the price you're paying for that payoff. For example, is it a coping mechanism that allows you to create distance between you and *your problems*? Is being "attached" taking up so much time and energy that it's keeping you from pursuing a worthy ideal or goal?

- What are healthier ways you can satisfy the need for importance, being needed, feeling connected, and so on?

- Write the name of someone whose difficulties you're taking on (or have recently taken on) as your own. In what ways can you support them by being committed, but not attached?

- While being committed but not attached can play out in a variety of situations, I chose to weave Paige's story throughout this life lesson. I'd like to say that if you're in a physically abusive relationship, it's *not* your fault. It's *never* your fault. *Ever.* Your partner needs help. *But so do you.* There are a variety of resources available, including hotlines, helplines, shelters, counseling, support groups, legal assistance, and websites dedicated to the awareness and prevention of domestic violence. Here are a few:
    - National Domestic Violence Hotline
        - Phone: 1-800-799-7233
        - Website: thehotline.org
    - Domestic Shelters
        - Offers a searchable database for shelters and services.
        - Website: domesticshelters.org
    - Women's Shelter Directory

- - Provides a comprehensive list of shelters across the US.
    - Website: womenshelters.org
  - Therapists and Counselors
    - Search for therapists who specialize in domestic violence.
    - Website: psychologytoday.com
  - Support Groups:
    - Al-Anon Family Groups, for those affected by someone else's drinking.
    - Website: al-anon.org
  - Legal Aid Society:
    - Offers legal assistance and information about domestic violence laws.
    - Website: legalaid.org
  - Domestic Violence Resource Center
    - Offers resources and support for those affected by domestic violence.
    - Phone: (24-hour crisis hotline) 1-866-469-8600
    - Website: dvrc-or.org

You Got This! Find the strength, resources, and support system to get away from an abusive environment. You'll be happy you made a better choice for *you*.

TWENTY-FIVE

WHEN YOU WALK OUT THE DOOR IN THE MORNING, NO ONE GIVES YOU A ROUND-TRIP TICKET

Trigger warning: This chapter contains examples of far-reaching tragedies that affected men, women, and children. My intention is not to sound morbid or depressing, but rather to support you in making amends and expressing your heartfelt gratitude while you still can. The thoughts and examples may bring up strong emotions, so please give consideration to the best time and place to read this chapter.

I'm sorry. Let's spend more time together. Please, let me explain what happened. It wasn't your fault. You're important to me. You changed my life. I'm so very proud of you. I may not have agreed with all your decisions, but I respect the choices you've made. I'll always be here for you. I was wrong. I only want the best for you. You're my inspiration. You're the best friend I've ever had. I'm glad you're my mom, you're the best. I couldn't have asked for a better daughter. You're the best thing that has ever happened to me. I let you down; you deserved better. Please forgive me. I admire you. I wasn't there for you. I wish I had it to do all over again. I'm glad you're my husband. Thank you. You're the best dad in the whole wide world. Can we try again? I couldn't have done it without you. I'm so happy you're my son. You were right. I want you back. I'd like us to be closer. I should have handled things differently. I want to make up for lost time. Thanks, Mom and Dad, for all the sacrifices you've made. I love you.

Is there something you've wanted or needed to say to your partner, parent, child, friend, mentor, colleague, or ex, but pride, fear, or an awkward moment has kept you from expressing it?

There's always tomorrow . . .

Not necessarily. When a 9.0 earthquake off the coast of Japan triggered a massive tsunami that reached nearly one hundred thirty feet in height, thousands of lives were lost. *There was no tomorrow.*

At Sandy Hook Elementary in Newtown, Connecticut, "tomorrow" vanished when a twenty-year-old gunman shot and killed twenty children and six staff members.

On September 11, 2001, *there was no tomorrow* for the thousands of victims in New York City. And for those they left behind, there were perhaps millions of words waiting to be spoken. The same words we *all* put on hold.

Say today what you may not have the chance to say tomorrow. Even if many months or years have passed, don't allow any possible shame or embarrassment to prolong the silence.

My colleague Darcy doesn't leave the house in the morning without first giving everyone a goodbye hug and a round of "I love yous." The last time she failed to do so was in high school, when she came home to learn that her dad had suffered a massive heart attack and died moments before she walked through the front door. For him, there was no tomorrow. And for Darcy, she would never share another tomorrow with her dad.

Getting real with people isn't always easy because it requires both courage and vulnerability, and for many of us, vulnerability is particularly daunting. But to connect with the people we love in a meaningful way, we need both. As one of my heroes, Brené Brown, contends, "There is no courage without vulnerability."

Yes, you risk something when you put yourself out there. But you stand to gain so much more, *and you stand to regret so much less.* Sincere words inspire. They heal. They're a bridge between yesterday and tomorrow. Between dissonance and harmony. And your words—spoken wholeheartedly—can change your relationships and the trajectory of your life.

ACTION STEPS:

- Identify one person with whom something has been left unsaid. This may include acknowledging the impact they've had on your life, apologizing, making amends, or expressing your heartfelt feelings toward them. Ask yourself, *If this were my last chance to speak with them, what would I most want to say? What would I regret not having said?*
- If you're feeling some resistance, what's the barrier? In other words, why haven't you said it yet?
    - If you were to keep that barrier in place, what do you see as being the best and worst case scenarios? And if you removed that barrier, and put yourself out there, what would be the benefit of doing so?
    - If you decide to verbalize what needs to be said (my recommendation 95 percent of the time), write it down. Think of this as a dress rehearsal. I said in a previous chapter that "ink makes us think." This step will help you articulate what you want to say, process what has held you back up until this point, and build

your courage and vulnerability muscle as you
work up to the real thing.

TWENTY-SIX

BEWARE OF GIRLFRIENDS WHO BAD-MOUTH GIRLFRIENDS ... AND PLEASE DON'T BECOME ONE OF THEM

When my daughter was a teenager, I had three rules when she was out and about with her friends:

1. Remember who you are.
2. If you *must* use a public restroom, don't go alone. Bring your friend. And for good measure, use two seat covers and flush with your foot!
3. Don't bad-mouth other girlfriends!

Though my daughter and her friends understood the virtues of the first two, I gently reminded them it was that third rule—if violated—that could wreak havoc on their relationships. Two things can—*and often do*—happen: The unkind remarks somehow meander their way to the person who was bad-mouthed, and the friend who is getting an earful has the nagging feeling that maybe, just maybe, she'll be the topic of one of your future lashings. Both storylines have detrimental outcomes.

Beware of girlfriends who bad-mouth girlfriends . . . *and please don't become one of them.* Aside from the fact that it's catty, it breaks down the trust. Your friend may start pulling away from you, either because she feels more devotion toward the one who's getting butchered, or she'll question *your* overall loyalty as a friend.

That's what happened between me and Amanda. We were having lunch one day when she started trash-talking Jessica, a mutual friend of ours. It wasn't the type of conversation born out of concern or even frustration. It was mean-spirited. I felt very uncomfortable, like it was an act of betrayal to be sitting there listening to it. My first thought was, *Wow, that's pretty vicious*, immediately followed by, *I wonder what she says about me when I'm not around.*

The person who gossips *to* you will gossip *about* you.

What made this even more unsettling was the fact that none of Amanda's negative feelings or opinions toward Jessica were even remotely visible when the three of us were together. Don't you hate it when you don't know where you stand with someone? Finally, when I could no longer take it, I said, "Amanda, if that's how you feel, you should really talk to Jessica about it." I added, "And I hope if you ever feel there's an issue between us, you'll discuss it face-to-face, so we can work through it." She got the point.

When it comes to backbiting, there's no such thing as an innocent bystander. It takes at least one person to talk and at least one person to listen. Although the listener may not have initiated the conversation, her willing participation fuels the fire, keeping the dialog alive. Any *Real Housewives* fan has seen this scenario play out time and again. It's a dynamic that emboldens the gossiper and gives her carte blanche to verbally vomit negative thoughts in a hurtful way—and to feel justified in doing so. Though I'm embarrassed to admit this, I've gotten sucked into the gossip vortex myself—as the gossiper because I had a need to vent, and as the "bystander" because it can happen so quickly, so subtly, that before we realize it, we're knee-deep in a conversation that can destroy a friendship, hurt our own reputation, and tarnish the character of the person we're smearing.

With so much fallout, why do we gossip? What's the allure? Here are a few responses I received to this question, some of which surprised me:

"It's a way for me to connect with other women, especially if I'm not feeling confident about my social skills."

"Sometimes I just have to get something off my chest."

"When someone is gossiping to me, I feel like they trust me."

"For some people, like me, it's a mechanism to build rapport. I know it's not healthy, but if you're insecure about your conversation skills, you go for the low-hanging fruit."

"Gossiping gives me a sense of superiority, especially when the other person agrees with what I'm saying. It makes me feel better about myself."

"Going with the gossip flow is easier than redirecting it."

"It's a way to bond with other women . . . but in a really unhealthy way."

"Someone isn't going to point out flaws in someone else that they also see in me, so it tells me they think more highly of me than the person we're gossiping about, at least in that particular area."

Regardless of the motivation to gossip, most of us would agree, it's a habit worth breaking. A quick way to turn things around, without sounding self-righteous, is to simply say, as I did to Amanda, "If it bothers you that much, you should talk to her about it." That sends a strong, yet non-confrontational, signal that you don't want to participate, while offering your friend a more positive alternative for resolving the issue. It also says loud and clear, *I'm the kind of friend who has your back. Someone you can trust—even when you're not around to hear what I'm saying.*

ACTION STEPS:

It's true, ladies, we like to talk when there's something on our mind. If it's good news, we want to share the joy and revel in the excitement with friends who echo our enthusiasm. On the flip side, when we're upset, we also need to talk. It helps us unburden the heaviness of our anger, frustrations, annoyance, and disappointment.

- So, try this: When you're feeling upset with one of your friends, journal about it.
  - First, write out—uncensored and unapologetically—every single thought and emotion that comes to mind related to the person and the situation that triggered you. This step is a brain dump. It's not meant to be Pulitzer Prize-winning prose. So no editing.
  - Next, take what you've written, using *select parts* of the brain dump, and turn it into a script; a letter to the friend who hurt, annoyed, or infuriated you. Here's the caveat: The goal of the letter is *not* to tell them off. The goal of the letter is *not* to be right. The goal of the letter is to *preserve the friendship.*
  - Next, sleep on it. You'll have new insights and a fresh outlook in the morning.

- o Revisit the letter and decide which talking points fit the criteria of not telling them off, but instead maintaining—even improving—the friendship. Is there something you'd like to say that would be best expressed in a different way? Is there something best left unsaid? Make your revisions.
  - o Now you're ready to encapsulate your talking points and have a well-articulated conversation.
- In the next chapter, "Confrontation Doesn't Have to Be Confrontational," I'll give you a six-step process to approach conflict in a positive way.

TWENTY-SEVEN

CONFRONTATION DOESN'T HAVE TO BE CONFRONTATIONAL

When my son, Michael, was a toddler, he would often accompany me in my volunteer work. One day I was working with a fellow volunteer named Ellie who was about fifteen years older than me and had "kids" in their late teens and early twenties. I could tell she was annoyed by my son's "spirited" demeanor. She made a few comments, and I immediately felt myself going into defense mode.

Although I would describe myself as "assertive," I sometimes find it necessary to tame the words stampeding across my brain. (Think: Spain's Running of the Bulls.) Through the years, I've developed a pretty good filter, which is undoubtedly congested with not-so-nice expressions that have kept me from getting fired, divorced, disowned, and flogged. My filter has proven invaluable throughout the years, as my thoughts—when I'm feeling attacked—should rarely go beyond my cerebral cortex.

So, here's what the stampede sounded like in my head: *You have a daughter on drugs, another who can't keep her knees together, and a son who won't talk to you. That hardly qualifies you as the poster child for Mother of the Year! Michael is a great kid! Who are you to judge him? Or me?*

Ouch! Heartless, I know. I know. I'm not proud that my thoughts even went there. Thank goodness my filter was on high alert and that venomous remark never made its way to my lips! As satisfying as it might have been in the moment to give Ellie a piece of my mind, I'm glad I didn't. In situations like that, the gratification is very short-lived and quickly replaced by regret and an urgent need to do the impossible: retract the spoken word. When we tell someone off—and especially when it's in a moment of anger—they usually feel hurt or become defensive, so it doesn't give them a chance to reevaluate what they've said. Plus, it puts a wedge in the relationship that only gets bigger with time.

Ellie must have realized later that week that she had been harsh and judgmental because she approached me saying, "It's a lot of work when your kids are little," and complimented me on what a great job I was doing. In the years that followed, she ended up being someone who gave me encouragement and motherly advice. I came to respect and admire her in many ways. Had I given in to my verbal inclinations, that never would have happened.

When it comes to confrontation, we usually overdo it (like I almost did!) or we steer clear of it altogether. The first extreme can damage the relationship. The second may reinforce an unhealthy pattern of avoidance behavior. Fortunately, there's a third option, and I've outlined it below. I've used this strategy in my personal and professional life, and I've been recommending it to clients for years. It takes the fear and awkwardness out of speaking up. *You Got This!*

Confrontation doesn't have to be confrontational. And it doesn't have to be something we avoid altogether. If we can look at conflict as a means to improve the relationship (and the situation), rather than an opportunity to read someone the riot act, we'll find that it's not so bad after all.

ACTION STEPS:

- Here's a six-step process that will allow you to be direct, avoid putting the other person on the defensive, and increase the likelihood of getting the result you want:

1. Start with something **positive** about them, related to the situation. And be authentic!
2. **Describe the behavior** that you're not happy with, being as specific as possible. Don't layer in your interpretation of what happened, just stick to the facts.
3. Express how you **feel** about what took place, using "I" statements. ("I feel . . ." *rather than* "You made me feel . . .") We don't want to put the other person on the defensive.
4. Let them know the **impact** of their behavior. (Yes, sometimes people need help "connecting the dots" between their behavior and the "drama-fications.")
5. Communicate what you would **like to see** happen, moving forward.
6. Then, tune into everyone's favorite radio station: WII-FM—What's In It For Me? In other words, relate how it will **benefit *them*** to change their behavior. This prompts the other person to be receptive, while making the desired shift more sustainable.

- Since this was a one-off scenario, I didn't see a need to confront Ellie. I would have, though, if the situation had persisted. Following the blueprint outlined above, it might have gone something like this:

Ellie, you have such a nice way of approaching people in our volunteer work. You're relatable and you ask engaging questions that make people think. I always learn something from you. I think it's important for Michael to learn at a young age to help other people and make a difference, so I usually have him with me. (Step #1) The last few times we've worked together you've said something negative about him. Just yesterday, you commented, "bla bla bla." And the week before, you said, "such and such." (Step #2) I'm upset because he's a great kid, and I work very hard to teach my children. A lot of it you don't see because it happens behind the scenes, at home. (Step #3) I'm at the point where I'm not looking forward to this, and neither is Michael, and I want a better experience for him. (Step #4) It would mean a lot to me if you would show him some patience and think back to when your kids were three years old. (Step #5) We'll both be more relaxed and we can use our energy to focus on the important work we're trying to accomplish. (Step #6)

- Remember, it's not just *what* we say, but *the way we say it*.
- I've outlined the steps as a template, which can make this read like a monologue. Be sure to leave space for back-and-forth conversation.
- Keep a friendly tone and begin with the end in mind: to change the behavior *and* keep the connection intact. Use it as a means to improve the relationship rather than an opportunity to tell someone off, and you'll increase the likelihood of a win-win outcome.

TWENTY-EIGHT

THE FAMILY PYRAMID

Every football season, my husband and I are invited to several Super Bowl parties. And every year, we politely decline all invitations. Except one: Super Bowl Sunday at my dad and Pat's. It's a given; a longstanding family tradition that —barring serious injury or an invitation to the White House —we're expected to commemorate. And truth be told, there's no other place the Holler "kids" would rather be. It's a reunion. A celebration. A reminder that the history we share is a seamless tapestry of inside jokes, awkward stages, and unforgettable experiences.

The six of us typically start texting across time zones in November. "Are you going?" The question needs no qualifier. No addendum. The meaning is clear: *Are you going to Daddy's for the Super Bowl this year?* For the Southern California locals, it's always a "yes." We wait for the final headcount as the out-of-towners reply, one by one.

Our siblings fly in from around the country as my dad and his wife, Pat, spend days cooking Italian food for dozens of friends and family—the "regulars" who have been faithfully coming for years. Neighbors, friends, and relatives who have had a front row seat to the milestones in our lives.

More than my dad's amazing baked rigatoni, and more than the camaraderie and competitive bantering that are inherently part of a good football game, what I look forward to most on the second Sunday in February is the Holler Family Pyramid. It's something we've been doing since our youngest sister was a preschooler. Now grown-ups, it has become a cherished ritual when we find ourselves in the same zip code. My two brothers, and whichever sister is the "sturdiest" at the time, get on all fours and establish the base. Then two. And one on top. By the way, the formation changes from year to year and is always accompanied by a "discussion" over who is thinner than whom and thereby unsuitable for the bottom. Ha!

Through the years, I've found myself on all three levels of the pyramid, both literally and figuratively: **The solid foundation:** The sister who is there for everyone; the pillar. **The top:** The one people look up to and admire. **And that second tier:** The one who is sandwiched in between the "wind" and the "wings." I didn't like it there. I felt displaced. *Replaced*, in some ways. But "replaced" would infer that I had proprietary rights in the sibling hierarchy. And that's not the case. Not for me. Not for any of us. Family dynamics change. *We* change. Yet we attach ourselves to familial roles like barnacles to a ship because they, in part, define who we are. And when that role changes, it's unsettling. It leaves a gap of uncertainty. At least it did for me. But I know now that the pyramid is only solid, resilient, and synergistic when we focus on each person's strengths instead of jockeying for position.

To borrow an example from nature, when geese fly in a V formation, they take turns being in front. This allows each goose to take the lead while the others recharge and take on more of a supportive role. While flying, they also "honk" to recognize and encourage the others to keep up the good work. We need to do the same.

Once we understand and appreciate each other's superpowers (as well as our own), we can forge stronger family bonds and work toward common goals and ideals.

Here's *my* Family Pyramid (aside from me) in order of appearance.

Frankie works hard, and he plays hard. He turns every occasion, every conversation, every interaction, into a side-splitting story—one to be retold and embellished throughout the years. As the family saying goes, "The party doesn't start until Frankie gets there." *Everyone* loves him! And what's *not* to love?

Traci is a fighter—*with a huge heart*—who has tackled every hardship and every challenge that has come her way. She's strong. She's self-reliant. Traci depends on no one, yet she supports *everyone*—especially her girls and grandkids. She has fierce determination, and I wish I had her tenacity!

We jokingly call **Bobby** "the eighty-year-old man." Wise beyond his years since his twenties, he's an old soul and my go-to sibling for sage advice. Of all of us, he's the only intro-vert, but the thoughts of his heart run deep and so does his character. I can't think of a single person in my life who has more integrity than my brother Bobby.

Saretta is incredibly talented in so many ways. She lights up every room she walks into, and while some people may like casting a shadow, Saretta never misses an opportunity to elevate the people around her, showcasing their talents and empowering and encouraging them to be their best. Her generosity is unmatched.

Jonika, she's the adventurer in the family. Whether skydiving, bungee jumping, cage diving with sharks, or trav-eling the world on a semester at sea, Jonika is always game for trying something new. Maybe that's why she's the most "chill" of all of us. *Nothing* stresses her out. As my husband will attest, I did not get that gene!

I love my sibling pyramid! But it took some soul-searching for me to realize it's okay to let someone else be the pillar. It took humility to appreciate that being in the spotlight for too long "blinds" us to everyone else's superpowers and doesn't leave room for someone else to shine. And it took some growing up to accept that when the "family pyramid" changes, *we* have the opportunity to change. To evolve. To support and be supported. To cheer for the person "on top." And most importantly, to appreciate that—through all the craziness, disagreements, imperfections, and unbreakable bonds of love—in the end, we make each other better.

ACTION STEPS:

- Think about *your* pyramid. It can be a family pyramid, work pyramid, or friendship pyramid. This is your community. Your "village." And, by the way, it doesn't have to neatly fit into a group of six. Define each person's superpowers by asking the others to write down three positive one-word attributes that best describe each person in the group. As you collect the data, look for common themes and recurring traits in each individual. These are their superpowers. *Your superpowers.*
    - At this point, you have unlimited options as to what you can do. Here are some possibilities: If you're focusing on your work team, you can incorporate this into a team-building activity. With friends and family, the top superpower(s) can be incorporated into a gift—possibly a personalized notebook, beverage mug, or a piece of jewelry.
    - Don't compete. Be unique. (More on this in chapter 36, "Run Your Own Race.") By nature of its design, this activity compels us to appreciate what each person in the pyramid

brings to the table. It's an acknowledgment, not a comparison. So it fosters a spirit of camaraderie and teamwork rather than a spirit of competition. We can be proud of others while still feeling proud of ourselves.
  - When we're dissatisfied with our lot in life, sometimes it's because we don't think we have "a lot" in life. This exercise will remind you of who you are, what people see in you, and the gifts that make you unique.
- To further promote a strong pyramid—or community—here are some questions to ask yourself that will help you embrace and leverage the role each person—including you—plays:
  - *Based on the superpowers of the others, what is something I can learn from each one of them?*
  - *Considering my collective strengths, in what ways can I support them in overcoming their challenges, achieving their goals, and following their dreams?*
  - *Where am I on the pyramid right now, and can any of us grow and become more self-aware if we "shifted positions" for a time?*
  - *Who needs to shine?*
  - *Who needs to offer support?*
  - *Who needs support?*
  - *Where are my gaps?*

TWENTY-NINE

FORGIVE YOUR PARENTS

A note before you read: Forgiving our parents can be complicated. Sometimes it's one of the most healing things we can do—and sometimes, it's not that simple.

This chapter is for women (and men) who want to repair or strengthen a relationship with a parent where there's still a foundation of love and safety, even if things feel strained or distant. Maybe there have been years of unspoken hurt, tension around big life choices, misunderstandings during stressful times, or emotional support you felt was missing when you needed it most.

If that sounds like your story—imperfect but salvageable —this chapter is for you.

But I want to be clear: If your experience involves abuse, abandonment, neglect, or deep estrangement, this life lesson is not meant to address that kind of pain. Those wounds run deep and often require the support of a trained mental health professional.

Forgiveness, like grieving, is a process—not a moment. It unfolds over time, and you're allowed to take it at your own pace. Trust your instincts. There's strength in knowing what you're ready for—and what you're not.

If this feels triggering, I encourage you to skip ahead to chapter 31. (Chapter 30, "Spend Time with Your Parents While They're Still Around," may also feel hard to take in.) You know what you need.

When my kids were little, from time to time I would playfully ask, "What's my favorite thing to be in the whole wide world?" With bright eyes and knowing smiles they would say in unison, "Our mommy!" As much as I love my kids (now adults), I'm sure I've made mistakes. My mom and dad did. Their parents did. It's inevitable.

I hope Madison and Michael forgive my shortcomings. After all, I've always had their best interests at heart. Most parents feel the same. Yet as an adult, possibly even a parent yourself, you may look back on your own childhood with sadness, even bitterness. I'm going to ask you to give your mom and dad some grace. If the hair on the back of your neck is sticking up, stay with me, and I'll explain more in a moment.

Forgive your parents. Not to excuse them, but to free yourself from carrying what was never yours to hold. Most parents did the best they could with the emotional tools and life experience they had. Who they are has been shaped by how they were raised, and how their parents were raised, and so on. To one degree or another, everyone's baggage is passed on to the next generation. What we choose to do with that "inheritance" is up to us. Still, don't throw the baby out with the bathwater. Take what was good. Embrace it. Pay it forward. And the painful parts? Reflect on them long enough to understand and grow. Sometimes we're the painter, adding color and dimension to the picture we were given. And sometimes we're the sculptor, carefully chipping away what no longer serves us.

Forgive your parents. Maybe they went through life-changing experiences that left deep scars, after which they were never quite the same. Imagine the effect that must have had on how they showed up for you. Forgiveness doesn't mean erasing the impact of their choices, but it can include empathy, compassion, and a desire to understand what shaped them. Search for that understanding—not to excuse, but to release. And sometimes, forgiveness includes setting boundaries—even with the people who raised us—especially if they haven't chosen to grow or heal themselves.

Forgive your parents. You may not like the fact that your mom constantly compared you to your brainiac sister. That was wrong. Hurtful. And I'm not excusing it. But maybe that's the thing that made you stronger. More tenacious. More determined to reach your goals. You may feel cheated because your dad was never around to play with you when you were a kid. If so, has that given you an unbreakable resolve to be an outstanding parent? Or, having made a conscious decision not to be flakey like your parents, do you now have a strong work ethic? Focusing on the lesson learned rather than *just* the culpability helps us take control of our life instead of feeling victimized by it.

Forgiveness is *not* synonymous with saying, "What you did was okay." Let me say that again because this is where a lot of people get stuck. Forgiveness is *not* the same thing as saying, "What you did was okay." I've seen men and women cling to their bitterness for years—sometimes even a lifetime—because they believe relinquishing it would trivialize the damage that's been done. Others think their mom or dad doesn't deserve their forgiveness. And maybe they *don't* deserve your forgiveness. I don't know. I wasn't there. But do *you* deserve to forgive them? Do *you* deserve to let go of it and move on with your life? I'd like to think so. It's been said that resentment is like drinking poison and expecting the *other person* to die. Forgiveness is not just something we give the other person. It's a gift we give ourselves. Letting go enables us to look forward, where we have a measure of control, rather than look back, where we have no power over what has already been done. Forgiveness gives us a sense of freedom. It allows us to let go of pain and anger. And it empowers us to be more aware of—and more gracious in accepting—our own imperfections. Give yourself the gift of letting go.

ACTION STEPS:

- If you're currently in the throes of a "situation" with your parents and clear boundaries are needed, please revisit chapter 23, "Invisible Boundaries Are Worse than No Boundaries at All," particularly the Action Step on setting *visible* boundaries, using the acronym BE CLEAR.
- Write down one thing you haven't forgiven your father or mother for. Even if you believe you've forgiven them, is there still a negative charge when you think about it? If so, write it down.
- Now, write a letter to him or her *that you have absolutely no intention of delivering.* There is nothing more intimate than what happens on the page. There's only you and your thoughts; your feelings —free of judgment, criticism, and repercussion. So be transparent. No one is going to read your words, except *you*. So the transparency is really for *your* benefit. Handwrite the letter. There is something cathartic about writing by hand, words and emotions flowing freely from your mind and heart to the page. Your handwriting is unique to you and you alone. It's the written manifestation of your DNA; a keyboard is not. Note each of the following steps before beginning your letter.
    - Start by telling the offending parent that you've been carrying something around for a while, it

has become heavy, and you're ready to release it.

- ○ Relate what he or she did that hurt you. Be specific. Give examples. You can go into as much detail as you'd like. Keep writing until you have it all down on paper.
- ○ Next, express how you feel/felt about what they did or did not do, using "I" statements— for example, "I feel angry/frustrated/sad." Taking responsibility for your feelings will help you let them go. You can't unburden something that isn't yours. So own it. "I feel . . ." instead of "You make me feel . . ."
- ○ Be clear about the impact their actions have had on your life and your relationship with them.
- ○ Articulate what you would like them to have done differently if they had a do-over.
- ○ Share at least one way in which this negative experience has made you a better parent, partner, leader, friend, or human being.
- ○ End with, "I'm not excusing what you did, but I'm forgiving you. I'm letting go of this because it no longer serves me and the people I love."

THIRTY

SPEND TIME WITH YOUR PARENTS WHILE THEY'RE STILL AROUND

Our biggest regrets will be those we can't reconcile—the losses that awaken us in the middle of the night wishing for a do-over and begging God to turn back the hands of time. Most of our feelings—joy, anger, love, sadness, jealousy—we can express. But what do we do with regret? It has nowhere to go because we yearn for something we might not get—a second chance.

Spend time with your parents. You don't know how much longer they'll be around. If you have ill feelings, make amends. If your life is too busy, either simplify or include them in the craziness.

In the 1989 film *Field of Dreams*, Kevin Costner portrays Ray Kinsella, an Iowa farmer who levels his cornfield and builds a regulation-size baseball field after hearing in a dream, "If you build it, he will come." Nostalgia sets in and baseball greats of days gone by, including Babe Ruth and "Shoeless" Joe Jackson, show up to play ball. Among the ghosts is Kinsella's father as he appeared in his early twenties—young, good-looking, guileless, with his whole life ahead of him—before the burdens of life crushed his spirit. It was a side his son was seeing for the very first time.

In a particularly moving scene, Kinsella plays a friendly game of catch with his dad—something he had longed to do since his father passed away. They bonded in a way they never had before. I remember sitting in the theater crying. My husband—who was my fiancé at the time—reminded me, as he always does, "It's only a movie, Lisa." I suppose that was the whole point: Kinsella actually had a chance to recreate the past—*something you can only do in the movies.* Back in the real world, there were people who would never have the opportunity to make things right with their mom or dad. That day, I was incredibly grateful I still had my parents. That we still talked and did lots of things together.

But time does not stand still.

On January 9, 2019, I lost my mom. There's really nothing that can prepare you for the death of a parent. It's surreal, even when you're expecting it.

If your mom or dad has passed away, then you know there's an overwhelming sense of loss. If you were close to your parents, the pain will eventually make way for reflective moments. But if you didn't spend much time together or if the relationship was strained, your grief might be accompanied by a deep sense of regret over what could have been.

If you have a relationship with your parents, spend time with them while they're still around. Laugh with them. Tease them. Tell them you love them. *Really* talk with them. Ask them about life; they've seen so much. Find out their most embarrassing moments. Their joys. Their disappointments. And their greatest achievements. Ask them to tell you funny stories about your childhood or about *their* childhood, so you can tell *your* kids one day. Ask for their help or advice; they still need to feel needed. Be with them. Love them. Help them. Connect with them.

When that gut-wrenching day comes and you have to say goodbye, the only things that will sustain you will be prayer, memories, and the people you love. If you made the most of your relationship with your mom and dad, the pain will eventually subside. But irreconcilable regret? That lasts a long time. Sometimes forever.

ACTION STEP:

- I recognize that not everyone has a healthy relationship with their parents. But if you do, here's an activity that will strengthen your connection and possibly outlive your parents *and* you: Pass a journal back and forth between you and one or both of your parents. In 2020, during the thick of the COVID-19 pandemic, I had this overwhelming urge to see my dad. To tell him how much I love him, to express something I couldn't quite identify. I showed up on his doorstep, choking back the emotion. The fear, the uncertainty, the social distancing, the isolation, the loss of my mom —it was all getting to me. Finally, through thick tears, I purged every thought and feeling I had been holding inside. On the other side of my meltdown emerged an idea: A writing project that my dad and I have come to simply refer to as "The Book." Two weeks later, I brought it to his house, with the following inscription:

Dear Daddy,
I'm excited to share this journey with you. Fifty-two weeks. Hundreds of insights, stories, emotions, and experiences. A couple of weeks ago, I left your house with two thoughts: One, I don't know how many years we have left together—but a lifetime isn't enough. And two, we both love words so let's work on a writing project together.
This is it . . .

I love you, Daddy!

I had purchased a spiral-bound journal and came up with fifty-two questions (one per week) that my dad and I would each respond to individually and then read together. Some of the questions are surfacy and fun; others go much deeper. I've listed the questions below. Feel free to approach them in any order. You may even decide to take out a few questions and replace them with some of your own. Through the pages of *your* Fifty-Two Weeks notebook, I hope something new and beautiful emerges in *your* relationships with your mom and dad. Enjoy the journey!

The questions:

- If your picture were on the cover of *Time* magazine, what would you want your legacy headline to be? Who do you have to show up as— every day—to make that headline a reality? (Three to four adjectives.)
- If you had one do-over in life, what would it be?
- Who is "the one you let get away?" In hindsight, do you think it would have worked out with them?
- If you could invite seven people whom you've never met—dead or alive—to a dinner party, who would you choose, and why?
- What personality trait are you most proud of?
- What talent are you most proud of?
- What was the best advice anyone ever gave you?
- Who, more than anyone else, helped shape you into the person you are today?
- What is the best compliment anyone has ever given you?
- What is a childhood memory that puts a smile on your face?

- What did you like best about your childhood? Your teens? Your twenties? Your thirties? What, if anything, would you change?
- Describe a time when you really felt a sense of belonging. Describe a time when you didn't.
- What are your favorite traits you got from your mom? What are your favorite traits you got from your dad?
- Who is the best friend you have ever had? What do/did you love and appreciate most about them? Tell a story of a special memory of them.
- Describe a time when someone really helped you out and gave you something you couldn't give yourself. How did you pay it forward?
- Who is someone in your life who hurt or disappointed you? How did you get beyond it, and what did you learn from the experience?
- If you could live anywhere on the planet for a year, and money wasn't an issue, where would you go? Why haven't you gone yet?
- Tell about a time you wish you would have handled something differently.
- What accomplishment are you most proud of?
- Who is the wisest person you've ever known, and if you had the chance, what would you ask them right now?
- What three things are you most grateful for?
- Write about a time you overcame a challenging situation. What did you learn about yourself?
- Tell me about a time you used a creative idea to get a specific result.
- If you were stranded on a desert island for two years and you could only take six books with you, what would they be, and why?
- What do you love most about me?

- If you had one do-over in your marriage, what would it be?
- If you had one do-over raising your kids, what would it be?
- If you had one career or academic do-over, what would it be?
- What do you fear most?
- What are the similarities between you and each of your kids?
- What are the top five things that bring you joy?
- What song title best describes your life, personality, or core beliefs?
- Write about a time you laughed really hard.
- Ask someone who knows you really well what five adjectives they would use to describe you. Do you agree? What's one adjective you would add to the list?
- What is the best vacation you've ever been on, and what made it special?
- Would you rather be admired or respected? Why?
- What would bother you more—to be disliked or to be misunderstood?
- What makes you happy? What would you say is the formula for happiness?
- Do you think you're more like your mom or your dad? What traits did you get from each that you especially appreciate?
- Describe a time when you felt special or important.
- What was one of your funniest or cutest one-liners as a kid that would be inappropriate or socially awkward to say as an adult?
- What is your favorite expression?
- If an actor/actress were to portray you in a major motion picture, who would you like to play that role, and why?

- What is one wish you have for me?
- What's your superpower?
- What is one talent you don't have that you wish you did? Why?
- If you were to choose a new career, what would it be?
- Tell about a time you showed grace and forgave someone. How were you able to finally let go of it? What did you learn about yourself in the process?
- Is there someone in your life who you haven't forgiven? If so, why not?
- Tell about a time you doubted yourself. What did you do to overcome your doubts?
- If you could live anywhere in the world, at any point in history, where and when would it be?
- If this were the last time we spoke, what would you want to tell me that you haven't already said?

PART THREE

STRIKE THREE DOESN'T
MEAN YOU'RE OUT

FOLLOW YOUR DREAMS

STEP INTO THE BEST
VERSION OF YOU

THIRTY-ONE

DON'T LOOK FOR A PERMANENT SOLUTION TO A TEMPORARY PROBLEM

Growing up, there were a few things that my strict East Coast Italian father did *not* want to see around the house: spaghetti sauce from a jar, the New York Knicks losing to the Boston Celtics, and any male interested in his teenage daughters. The latter posed a real problem for me.

It was my sophomore year in high school and there was this dance I really wanted to attend. I had asked my father (begged, actually) months in advance if I could go. That would give him plenty of time to meet my date and see for himself that he was a nice guy. Unfortunately, my dad considered "nice guy" to be a contradiction in terms. Two weeks before the dance, he announced the decision he likely had made three and a half seconds after I made my initial request: "You're not going. Guys just want one thing!"

What? Where did that come from? It's just a dance. How could he do this to me? Ugh . . . He just doesn't want me to have any fun. That's it! I'm running away.

My life (all fifteen years of it) was over!

In short, I couldn't see beyond the present situation. Guess what? We do the same thing as adults. The stakes may be higher, but the mindset is the same: When we feel overwhelmed by work, school, relationships, and our emotions, we blow challenges, problems, and disappointments out of proportion. When that happens, we can't see the answer, even when it's right in front of us. We start looking for a permanent solution—something extreme or irreversible—to a temporary problem. We act out with destructive behaviors. We say hurtful things we may later regret. We divorce instead of going to counseling. We file for bankruptcy rather than get reliable financial advice. We quit our job before trying to settle things with our boss or colleagues. We marry someone we've settled for instead of holding out for the right one. And we sever ties with people we care about in lieu of swallowing our pride and working through our differences.

Don't look for a permanent solution to a temporary problem. Why amputate your finger when a Band-Aid will do the trick?

Whenever my mom faced what seemed to be insurmountable challenges, her mom would remind her, "It's only temporary, Norma." I'm grateful to Grandma Libby for passing down that perspective. When we start viewing problems and challenges as "permanent," finding an answer becomes much more difficult. There's a heaviness to it. We have very little motivation to change the situation because the answers feel outside our reach and we can't see the light at the end of the tunnel. But if we can view trials as temporary, it's easier to wrap our mind around a results-oriented solution—a step-by-step game plan to get us from A to Z. More often than not, as we break down the problem, the challenge, or the decision, we find it's not as overwhelming as we had initially thought.

The dance was one of many fleeting disappointments in my life. My dad and I laugh about it now, but I was devastated back then. True, we may not always reflect on hard times with a smile, but if we can realize *most* challenges are only temporary, we can work our way through them, rather than become overwhelmed by them.

ACTION STEPS:

- Identify a previous—seemingly insurmountable—challenge that you overcame, a "temporary" problem that seemed "permanent" at the time.
  - What personal characteristics helped you to overcome that challenge? Was it your grit? Your insightfulness? Your optimism? Your creativity? Something else? Your superpowers become stronger with use, and they're here to serve you once again!
- What challenging circumstances are you facing now? Or is there a tough situation on the horizon?
  - Let's get ahead of it. How can you put your superpowers to good use?
  - Who in your tribe can you count on for support and encouragement? If it's a small tribe, that's okay. The quality of your tribe—their integrity, commitment, and love for you—is much more important than the size.
  - How do you eat an elephant? One bite at a time! That being said, ask yourself, *What's one step I can take this week (even today) that will have a positive impact on my situation—before I feel compelled to resort to a "permanent" solution?*
  - Fast-forward your life twenty years into the future. What advice or encouragement would you give your younger self regarding this "temporary" problem? Life always looks different in the rearview mirror!

THIRTY-TWO

SAY "THANK YOU" TO LIFE'S DISAPPOINTMENTS

Country western superstar Garth Brooks has a gift for recording songs with a message about life. "Unanswered Prayers" is no exception. The song begins at his class reunion where he sees his high school flame and reflects on his request that "God would make her mine." As the story unfolds, he realizes that his *wife* is his greatest blessing, while the woman he had hoped for, dreamed about, and prayed would be his in his younger years, didn't quite measure up to his illusions. It's a feel-good, put-a-smile-on-your-face song with an important lesson: Sometimes we need to say "thank you" to life's disappointments. Now and then, what we had wished for isn't what would have been best for us in the long run.

Consider Vera Wang. Before she became a world-renowned designer, her dream was to compete as an Olympic figure skater. When she didn't make the US team, it was crushing. But that disappointment redirected her path. She moved into fashion, and eventually created one of the most recognizable names in modern bridal and couture. Sometimes the door that closes is the one that sends you where you were meant to go.

In a similar twist of fortuity, Evan Williams launched the podcast platform Odeo. Shortly thereafter, Apple announced its podcasting platform, dramatically altering Odeo's trajectory. Disappointing? Yes! Frustrating? Absolutely! A dead end? Not by any means. Williams pivoted and went on to cofound Twitter (now X), radically transforming microblogging. In the end, Williams was grateful that Odeo did not succeed as planned. Serendipitous turns can often lead to unexpected—and more favorable—outcomes. Say "thank you" to unanswered prayers!

It's easier to accept disappointment once we understand that our wish, our dream, is like a blank sheet of paper waiting to be filled: We write the script. We create the fairytale ending. Each detail is crafted to perfection. Our imagination, which almost always trumps reality, is the author. It's so easy to project all the good, conveniently leaving out the imperfections that are woven throughout the tapestry of *real* life.

I'm not minimizing the way it feels when we don't receive the job offer we desperately wanted, when we open the rejection letter from our top college pick, when we don't get the house that we put an offer on, or when things don't work out with the guy whose last name we doodled endlessly next to ours. But do any of us really know how the job, the school, the neighborhood, the relationship (fill in the blank) would have turned out, had it come to fruition? Or are we projecting onto that blank sheet of paper? Is it possible that something even better is just around the corner?

Sometimes disappointments end up working out for the best. We just can't see it at the time. So when life lets you down, have a little faith. Don't swim in the disappointment of what could have been. Instead, move on with your eyes wide open so you can see the opportunities waiting to be discovered, created, and embraced.

ACTION STEP:

- Try this: When things don't turn out as planned, give yourself a predetermined time frame in which you get to be angry, feel sorry for yourself, cry, journal about it, and vent to your girlfriends. Then say "thank you" and move on. Doing so keeps you from exhausting your energy on something you can't change. More importantly, it leaves you mentally and emotionally open to other possibilities.

THIRTY-THREE

THERE ARE TWO THINGS YOU CAN COUNT ON—YOURSELF AND YOUR FINGERS . . . AND ONE OF THEM YOU STOPPED USING IN THE SECOND GRADE

I've never considered myself a cynical person. But one evening in Atlanta, Georgia, circa 1988, something shifted.

Russia had temporarily added baseball to its lineup of professional sports. In preparation for the upcoming Olympics, Russia's premier baseball team came to the United States to play the best colleges in the country. I was working in the public affairs department at Taco Bell—the title sponsor for the tour. My task: to travel the southern United States with the team, conducting media interviews and coaching the players on how to comment to the press. At the time, Taco Bell was a subsidiary of PepsiCo, Inc. There would be lots of cameras and lots of reporters. So before catching a flight to North Carolina, my boss gave me a final reminder: "Lisa, make sure the guys have Taco Bell and Pepsi products *at all times.*"

Not a problem until we arrived in Atlanta, Georgia— home of Coca-Cola.

The rivalry between Pepsi and Coke was fierce. For over 100 years, the two major players in the beverage industry had vied for increased market share. And in Atlanta, the town looked after its own. It was nearly impossible to track down Pepsi in the Coke capital of the world. But I was on a mission! I had to find a way to make it happen. It would have been embarrassing, to say the least, for the title sponsor to be upstaged by its competitor. The press would have had a field day.

Taco Bell had hired an outside marketing firm to assist with promotions. In a few short hours, we would be hosting a media event at a restaurant in Atlanta. Among those scheduled to attend were the network affiliates. I brought the marketing folks up to speed on the Pepsi-Coke scenario and reminded them to make certain all beverages were served in restaurant glasses, not logo-adorned Coke cans. I continued my search for Pepsi and would be joining them shortly.

Big mistake!

When I arrived at the media event, Pepsi in hand, two things simultaneously caught my eye and nearly stopped my heart: Coke cans were on every table in the restaurant *and* a camera crew was walking out the front door—which could only mean they had already captured the footage needed for the story. *This is not good, Lisa. Russian baseball players drinking America's number one soft drink? No self-respecting journalist would miss that one!* I followed the crew out to their production van (actually, I darted, frantically) and I asked in my sugariest tone of voice if I could please see their footage. (I may not have the same charm as a Southern belle, but with two parents from Brooklyn, I've learned to talk my way out of almost anything!)

Sure enough, the soon-to-air segment began with a tight shot of the legendary red and white Coke logo, widening out to include two Russian baseball players drinking the soda and obviously enjoying themselves. *Great. Can it possibly get any worse?* Yep. Every three seconds, another can of Coke popped onto the screen.

At Taco Bell headquarters in Irvine, California, no employee would ever dream of bringing Coke into the building unless, of course, he or she was particularly fond of the mailroom . . . or the unemployment line. My transgression went far beyond that.

After explaining to the cameramen that I would not have a job on Monday if the spot aired as-is on the eleven o'clock news, they promised they would edit around the Coca-Cola footage.

I learned an important lesson that day: There are two things you can count on— yourself and your fingers. And one of them you stopped using in the second grade. Certain things you just don't delegate. Yes, there are times when you have to rely on competent people. But ask yourself, *What is the worst thing that could happen if they were to drop the ball?* Consider the potential consequences and choose wisely.

I didn't have a moment of peace until I watched the eleven o'clock news that evening. As I anxiously turned on the television in my hotel room, I hoped for the best and braced myself for the worst. Then, I breathed a sigh of relief. There was no close-up of a Coke can. No Coke products at all. *Yes! I would still be gainfully employed on Monday.*

I never shared this near faux pas with my boss. But I suppose he's bound to hear about it now. *Sorry, Elliot.*

ACTION STEPS:

- When running point on any type of professional, social, organizational, or community project, identify potential challenges and have a contingency plan.
- Delegate strategically. If you can't take the hit, *do it yourself.*

THIRTY-FOUR

IT'S NOT ABOUT THE CARDS WE'VE BEEN DEALT —IT'S HOW WE PLAY OUT OUR HAND THAT COUNTS

Life isn't perfect. And it isn't always beautiful. The beauty lies not in the circumstances but in the way we choose to deal with, and rise above, those circumstances. It comes down to this: In the game of life, it's not about the cards we've been dealt; very few have been given a royal flush. It's how we play out our hand that counts.

There's a powerful lesson to be learned from the strength and adaptability of trees. In forest ecosystems worldwide, research has shown that trees exposed to repeated winds often develop thicker trunks and deeper root systems. *They grow through adversity!* And while harsh conditions can be damaging in the *short term*, trees that withstand inclement weather often emerge healthier and more resilient. *The same is true with people.* Like the tree that becomes deeply rooted after the storm, allow the adversities of life to reveal your strength, and depth, and beauty.

Some people don't just rise above their setbacks—they build something lasting from them. They take their pain and turn it into purpose. On the other side of the world, nearly two centuries ago, a three-year-old boy lost his eyesight in a freak accident while playing with his father's tools. He faced a future filled with enormous obstacles, especially when it came to getting an education. But he was determined not to let his blindness stop him—or others like him. At just fifteen, he invented a system of raised dots that blind and visually impaired people could use to read and write with their fingertips. That system would go on to open doors to education and independence for millions of people around the world. His name? Louis Braille.

Make a choice today to make the most of your circumstances. The setbacks you're experiencing are temporary.

Life isn't always easy, and it certainly isn't fair. But we don't have to be defined by the realities we were born into. And we don't have to be limited by the circumstances that landed—*uninvited and unwelcome*—at our doorstep.

Oprah Winfrey is living proof that where you start—or where you are right now—isn't where you have to stay. Born into poverty in rural Mississippi, she suffered neglect, instability, and physical and sexual abuse. She became pregnant by one of her abusers when she was fourteen, giving birth to a son who tragically died only weeks later. The deck was stacked against her. But she didn't fold. Instead, driven by grit, determination, and empathy, she became a philanthropist, a media mogul, and the face of personal empowerment, rising to become one of the wealthiest and most influential women in the world.

Oprah endured extreme hardship and still created a life of purpose and joy. Her journey is a powerful reminder that healing is possible—and so is happiness, no matter where you're starting from. What might it look like for you to begin that journey?

In the midst of all those setbacks, when Oprah may have wanted to give up, do you think she had any idea of the enormous impact she would eventually make? I'm not sure. The real question is, *Are you aware of the kind of impact that you are capable of making?* I hope so. But here's the thing: You can't always see your full potential until you've made it through the hard stuff—not by powering through it alone, but by facing it with courage, support, and a deep belief that your story isn't over yet. It's about showing up one appointment, one conversation, one decision at a time.

- It's the college student struggling with anxiety who still shows up to class, even if she has to sit in the back with a quiet exit plan.
- It's the entrepreneur who's not sure how to fund the next phase of her business, but she sends out one email, makes one call, pitches one idea anyway.
- It's the woman who's been knocked down by life more times than she can count—but still gets up.

Remember, empowerment doesn't always look like a bold leap. Sometimes it's just choosing not to give up on yourself, even when you're tired, scared, or unsure. Each time you choose not to let your past define your future, each time you ask for help, set a boundary, or take one small step forward, you're reshaping your life. You're playing your hand with strength, even when the cards aren't perfect. And *that's* how the game is won.

ACTION STEPS:

- Attitude is one of the few things in life over which we have total control. Although you may have every right to feel sorry for yourself, put limits on this—simply because it won't improve your situation. I don't want to sound unsympathetic. I just want you to use your energy in a way that helps you heal rather than allowing the wounds to fester.

- Instead of complaining about the "cards" you've been dealt, denying the existence of a bad situation, or simply positive affirmation-ing your way out of it, try this:
    - Acknowledge the hand you've been dealt. You can't improve on anything without first being fully aware of what you're up against.
    - Ask yourself, *What part of this is in my control and what is out of my control?* What resources do I need to improve my situation? And will any of those resources bump something from the out-of-my-control category to the in-my-control category?
    - Now, focusing on what you have control over, write a list of ten things you can do to improve your circumstances.
    - Next, identify the one thing on your list that will have the biggest impact. That's your starting point. Continue to fine-tune and implement your action items. Being proactive will make your challenges appear smaller because you're gradually shifting your focus from problems to solutions. You'll start feeling more empowered and less victimized.
- As I mentioned earlier, I've peppered goal-setting Action Steps (all slightly different) throughout the book. Nothing catapults us out of the doldrums and into the game faster than setting a goal that lights us up! It doesn't matter what the goal is, as long as it's important to *you*. To get started, determine your five Ws: who, what, where, when, and why.

- **Who: Who** do you want to be? In other words, if people were to describe you, what traits would you most like to hear? Write them down. What adjustments do you need to make in order to authentically show up as that person? Be honest with yourself. As I touched on in the introduction, we can't get to where we're going without first looking at who we're being.
- **What: What** is a worthy goal that would get you excited about getting out of bed in the morning?
- **Where:** All journeys begin with a point of departure. Determine *where* you are now and be *where* you want to land. Be specific about your starting point and have a clear vision of how that goal will look and feel when achieved. Describe both in detail. Then, recite your vision out loud and share it with someone you trust. Studies show that writing *and* verbalizing our goals increase our commitment, motivation, and accountability. In fact, a study published in the *Journal of Applied Psychology* noted that people who wrote down and vocalized their goals were much likelier to achieve them, compared to those who just thought about them.
- **When:** By **when** do you want to achieve this goal? It's important to date-stamp our aspirations. This keeps us on track, gives us a sense of urgency, and helps prevent an acute case of "excusitis." Sometimes a "when" can seem too far off in the distant future. So chunk it out and break your objective down into smaller goals. And yes, celebrate your successes along the way! Acknowledging your progress

will build confidence and spark your desire to continue—even when it's hard. One day, you'll wake up to find that the road leading to the finish line is shorter than the one traveled. And that's pretty exciting!

- **Why: Why** is achieving this goal important to you? I'm a big Simon Sinek fan. According to the bestselling author of *Start with Why*, understanding the why behind our goal will give us motivation, resilience, consistency in decision-making, clarity of purpose, and long-term fulfillment.

- Find your tribe—like-minded people who respect, care about, support, and understand you. If you're new to the area or you're still building your support system, consider places of worship, work, school, hobby-related classes, volunteering, and organizations that make a difference. This is where you'll find people with similar values, goals, talents, passions, and purposes.

- Align yourself with people who focus on how they can *improve* their situation rather than those who habitually feel victimized by their circumstances.

THIRTY-FIVE

IF YOU WANT TO GET YOUR FOOT IN THE DOOR, HAVE A LITTLE MOXIE

Moxie: energy, pep, courage, determination, know-how, spunk.

Week one: It was the fifth time I had called in the last five days. It was also the fifth time he politely informed me that Mr. Harris was in a meeting. *Yeah, right.*

Week two: A repeat of week one. If nothing else, college taught me this: *If at first you don't succeed, change your strategy, Lisa!*

I had just graduated with a degree in broadcast journalism, and I wanted to be the next reporter at a small television station in Santa Barbara, California. *If only I could get the news director, King Harris, on the phone.* But his well-trained gatekeepers repeatedly informed me, "He's in a meeting" or "We're not hiring any reporters right now, so he probably won't even call you back."

Hmm . . . We'll see about that.

Week three: I FedExed the news director my résumé, *a brand-new shoe*, and a note that read:

JUST WANTED TO GET A FOOT IN THE DOOR

Mr. Harris,

I will be in Santa Barbara next week. I've made a reservation for noon on Tuesday at a local restaurant. I would like to take you to lunch and give you my audition materials in person. I'll call you within the next two days to confirm.
I look forward to meeting you!

The following day: Once again—and with a renewed sense of confidence, I might add—I dialed the number that was now permanently embedded in my brain. I heard that well-rehearsed and all-too-familiar response, "I'm sorry, he's in a meeting right now."

I gave the gatekeeper my name, adding that I had overnighted Mr. Harris a package and wanted to confirm that he received it. That's when the conversation took a positive turn. "You're the girl with the foot in the door!" he blurted out. "We've been talking about it all morning! That shoe thing was great! Hold on. I'll get him on the phone."

Week four: I was sitting at the television station with the news director and one of his reporters. Although they had no openings at the time, they spent an hour with me reviewing my audition materials and offering advice on breaking into the business—a rare courtesy in television news.

While I never anchored the six o'clock news, I did go on to work in public relations for a Fortune 500 company, moved on to coaching and workshop facilitation, and eventually pursued my dream of becoming an author. Having a little moxie has helped me every step of the way. And I have my mother and grandmother to thank. They *both* had moxie!

We live in a competitive world. Women vie for scholarships, for jobs, for promotions. For a seat at the table. Ordinary measures will get you ordinary results.

If you want to stand out, have a little moxie. Don't be afraid to put yourself out there, to be unique, to be a little daring. It shows confidence and a passion for what you're pursuing. Get creative; think outside the box. It won't bring world peace. And it may not cure cancer. But it just might help you get a foot in the door!

ACTION STEP:

- When Moxie 1.0 gets your "foot in the door," but doesn't quite land you the job (or whatever else you've set your sights on), elevate to Moxie 2.0. I've wished so many times that I would have taken that leap. Moxie 2.0 requires *a lot* of confidence, an unwavering belief in yourself, and (male or female) some pretty big balls. In my mid-twenties, I wasn't quite there yet. But I'm really rooting for you to be there, much sooner than I was! And if you're not, fake it till you make it. In the newsroom situation, after meeting with King Harris, Moxie 2.0 would have sounded something like this:

Mr. Harris, hire me. I know you don't have any openings right now for a reporter. That's okay. I'll run errands. I'll do grunt work. But I'll also generate story ideas. I'll learn everything there is to learn about television news. And when you're ready to hire another reporter, I will have already demonstrated my abilities. Just like I got my foot in the door with a shoe, I'll open other doors in central California—doors that lead to compelling and captivating stories. And I'll do it by being creative, tenacious, smart, and charming. I know I belong here. You just don't know it yet. But you will. I promise.

THIRTY-SIX

RUN YOUR OWN RACE

When thoroughbreds run a race, some wear blinkers, also known as blinders. This keeps them from getting distracted by horses galloping on either side of them. The practice, believed to have dated back to ancient Greece, restricts their peripheral vision, forcing them to concentrate on the goal ahead. In short, blinkers keep the horse focused on running a successful race, unencumbered by everyone and everything around them. Just imagine Secretariat, one of the most celebrated racehorses of all time, glancing over at one of his competitors, sizing them up and becoming either overconfident, discouraged, intimidated, or spooked by the hand-flailing, noisy crowd. There's a lesson here: Run your own race.

Years ago, I accepted the fact that there would *always* be someone smarter than me. Prettier than me. More creative than I am. A better writer. A better speaker. And the list goes on and on. So I decided not to compete against them, but instead to compete against myself. As long as I continued to raise the bar, stay the course, and "run" with passion and determination, I could be the best version of me. When we compete against someone else, that doesn't always happen.

Running your own race forces you to play to your

strengths. I was reminded of this in 2010 when I was competing for a coveted spot with a top-tier professional development company. I was surrounded by some serious talent! Each time I compared myself to the competition, I came up short: There were high-level executives; business consultants with global training experience; accomplished professionals who had more initials after their name than I did; a polished college professor who had previously anchored the six o'clock news. *What am I doing here?* I felt intimidated. And even though I put on a good front, inside I felt like I didn't quite measure up. I knew it would only be a matter of time before everyone else—including the powers that be—came to the same conclusion.

I was so busy admiring (and coveting) everyone else's superpowers, I wasn't able to see what I could bring to the table. That's when my sister, Saretta, also in the running, reminded me that the company wasn't necessarily looking for people with the most impressive résumés. They were in the "relationships" business. They wanted trainers who were great communicators, had strong people skills, and were passionate about making a difference. That was me! That was my sweet spot! I loved people, and communication was my jam! I didn't have to compete against the other candidates. I just needed to put on the blinders, play to my strengths, and compete against myself. I needed to run my own race! From that moment on, that's what I did, and I felt like this heavy weight had been lifted from my shoulders. Among the forty-five contenders, my sister and I were two of the four who made it to the "finish line." The "run your own race" approach worked for me and I know it can work for you too!

ACTION STEPS:

- Instead of trying to be a better version of someone else, be unique. Don't compete. After all, what's more profound and satisfying—being an upgraded carbon copy of someone else, or the best possible version of you?

- Write down the three qualities, skills, or talents that you are most proud of. Then ask five people, who know you well, for three positive qualities, skills, or talents that best describe you. You'll likely notice three to five recurring themes. These are your superpowers. Write each superpower on an index card. The next time you're tempted to compete with someone other than yourself, take out one or more of those cards and ask yourself, *How will this quality, skill, or talent help me present myself in a powerful and creative way? How can my ability to (fill in the blank) differentiate me while having a profound impact on other people? In what ways can I use this superpower to create the result I'm looking for?* Compare how you feel when competing against others to how you feel competing against yourself. Pay special attention to the energy *experienced* and the energy *expended*. What were your insights?

- Exploring your motives can be just the right catalyst for personal growth. Ask yourself, *Am I comparing myself to others because I'm running a race for someone else—for example, parental approval, social status, or societal expectations?*

- Commit to leveling up, to being a better you today than you were yesterday. Rinse and repeat.

THIRTY-SEVEN

IF YOU WANT TO BE GOOD, YOU HAVE TO LET GO OF LOOKING GOOD

This is going to sound counterintuitive, but if you want to be good—I mean really good at something, something that you're passionate about—you're going to have to let go of *looking good*. Looking good is the nemesis of risk-taking, creativity, and growth. When you're hyper-focused on what people think of you, you're not going to "color outside the lines" and test the boundaries of your potential. Instead, you'll play it safe.

Looking good is all about what other people think of you. *Being good* is all about what you think of yourself. It's deeply rooted in your desire to have a meaningful impact on the world and the people around you. If you're afraid that others might judge you, let me obliterate the uncertainty. They will! But assuming that your character and integrity are intact, what people think of you is far less important than what you think of yourself.

Part of my role as a personal and professional development coach is to help people get comfortable being uncomfortable. I was facilitating a communications workshop where each participant was asked to take a significant step outside their comfort zone in order to achieve the desired result:

increased self-confidence and greater bandwidth as an influential communicator. I could see the hesitation around the room. For some, the fear was palpable. It was time for The Speech: "By a show of hands, how many of us are feeling uncomfortable right now?" (Lots of hands.) "Perfect. You're exactly where you need to be because you can only grow *outside* your comfort zone. How many of us are convinced that we're going to look really foolish if we do this exercise?" (More hands.) "What happens here in this training is a microcosm of what happens out there at work and in your personal life. If you're holding back right now and not playing full out because you're worried about how you might look, or there's a fear of being judged, guess what? You're also holding back in life, where it matters most. *If you want to be good, you've got to let go of looking good!* You're afraid someone might laugh at your ideas? Your invention? Your opinions? Your dreams? Put it out there anyway. Some of the so-called "craziest" ideas in history have transformed the technology, transportation, communications, medical, and entertainment industries. Are you playing it safe, never challenging yourself? Knock that off! You're all here because you want to be a better version of yourself. And in order for that to happen, you've got to let go of the fear of being judged. I'll say it again: Don't give your power away. *If you want to be good, you have to let go of looking good.*"

They continued the exercise with a newfound perspective. They *completed* the exercise feeling more self-confident and less self-conscious. Most importantly, as the weeks and months progressed, they leveled up and experienced unprecedented breakthroughs. They ventured into exciting—and sometimes unfamiliar—terrain because they had the courage to do it scared and let go of looking good.

Think about some of the most influential innovators of our time, and those who blazed a trail before them: Elon Musk, Steve Jobs, Mark Zuckerberg, Sheryl Sandberg, Albert Einstein, Thomas Edison, Marie Curie, the Wright brothers,

Nikola Tesla, and so many others. Their strokes of genius could not have been manifested within the boundaries of looking good. Here's the irony—they focused on *being good,* and in the end, they also *looked good.* This does not work in reverse. Being good has to be the motivating factor.

The road to self-discovery, fulfillment, success, contribution, and self-acceptance is paved with judgment and failure. But failure is not the opposite of success; it's simply part of the process. Looking good might be the path of least resistance, but there's a cost: relinquishing control of your life; giving your power away; surrendering who you are. So it's worth asking, *Do I really want someone else to be the architect of my future?*

ACTION STEP:

- Nike had it right when they immortalized the slogan, "Just Do It." Every day, for the next thirty days, do something that's outside of your comfort zone. Here are some ideas:
  - Volunteer to take the lead on a project.
  - If giving a speech or a presentation feels scarier than a root canal, do it anyway.
  - Have a much-needed, difficult conversation with a neighbor, coworker, family member, or friend. (Revisit chapter 27 for a few tips.)
  - Smile and say hello to someone you think is attractive or even out of your league.
  - If you have a fear of drowning, take swimming lessons.
  - Offer a cost-saving or time-saving idea to someone at your company in a senior leadership position.
  - Chat with the grocery checker, barista, or person you're standing next to in line.

There are two rules:

1. Be safe. Use sound judgment. For example, don't run across the freeway or experiment with recreational drugs. The goal is personal growth, not a trip to the hospital.
2. Don't be tied to the outcome. For example, if you choose to smile and say hello to someone you think is attractive or even out of your league, don't look at it as a failure if the person doesn't ask you out on a date. It's not about the result. You're building the muscle of getting comfortable being uncomfortable. *That's it.*

THIRTY-EIGHT

"IMPOSSIBLE" SIMPLY MEANS IT HASN'T BEEN DONE YET

Somewhere between ambition and fruition lie passion, hard work, and an unwavering belief in ourselves. Of the three, none is more vulnerable than the latter because we may unwittingly allow other people to question our ability to accomplish remarkable things. Worse yet, we may start believing them. When that happens, we begin to see our goals, and ourselves, through someone else's lens—a perspective that may be tainted with their own self-doubt, negativity, even jealousy.

Dream big. And when you do, be selective about who you share those dreams with. Here's why: As we set our goals—and begin talking about them—we encounter three types of people:

1. **Cheerleaders:** These are the people we want in our circle—the friends, family members, and colleagues who believe in us and champion our aspirations.
2. **Naysayers:** These are the "friends," family members, and colleagues who may laugh in our

face, snort disparagingly, call us a dreamer, or say,
"That's impossible."

3. **Room Temps:** These are the people who are
   neither hot nor cold; the ones who may respond
   with a shrug and a passive "Oh, that's nice." They
   aren't inspired or intrigued by what we're up to,
   but they aren't actively discouraging or dissuading
   us from moving forward.

To the number twos of the world (pun intended), I say,
"Impossible" simply means it hasn't been done yet.

Find your "cheerleaders." I'm not talking about people
who praise your work or your ideas simply for the sake of
being nice. I'm talking about the people who have faith in you,
feel inspired by you, see the best *in you*, and want the best *for
you*. Have cheerleaders in your life and be that cheerleader for
other women.

When someone believes in us, it validates who we are.
When we feel validated, we take greater risks. When we take
greater risks, our comfort zone expands and we become more
confident. As our confidence grows, we develop a stronger,
more resolute belief in ourselves. And the cycle continues.
This is why "cheerleaders" are such a positive force in our
lives.

On the other hand, when a well-meaning friend raises a
judgmental eyebrow and says, "Really?" we may be tempted
to mirror their doubts. But remember—and this is important
—they are speaking from *their* frame of reference. It's not an
absolute truth and it's not necessarily a reflection of *you*. Let
me give you an example: If they were raised in a home where
goals were not encouraged, they may have no foundation for
believing that anything extraordinary is possible. Jealousy is
another factor that comes into play. You have the guts to
follow your dream. And the guts to fail. Quite frankly, maybe
they don't. Regardless, don't let negativity or indifference rob

you of your dream. If you do, it will alter who you could have become and will preclude the contribution you could have made.

In fact, here are some major accomplishments that were previously deemed "impossible:"

- The invention of the airplane by the Wright brothers in 1903.
- Breaking the four-minute mile for distance running in 1954.
- The moon landing in 1969 when astronauts Neil Armstrong and Buzz Aldrin took "one small step for man, one giant leap for mankind."
- April 30, 1993, when the World Wide Web was introduced into the public domain and changed the way we connected and communicated.

And consider this: If every writer chose not to play the publishing odds, countless classics would have remained unknown to the world. If every teenager with a guitar, or a piano, or even a tune in their head concluded that his or her dreams were too lofty, we would live in a world void of music. If brilliant minds and innate curiosity were halted by discouraging voices, Apple would only be known as a fruit instead of one of the most recognizable brands in the world.

Your dreams don't have to change the world (although they can). Would you like to be the first person in your family to attend and graduate from college? Do you have a disabled child who—so far—has been denied important resources? Will overcoming certain challenges mean that you can be a teacher? A doctor? A voice in your community?

Don't impose—or allow others to impose—limits on you or the people you love. The next time someone says, "Um, you're setting your sights a bit high, don't you think?" Remember this: *Someone* has to do it. Why shouldn't it be *you*?

ACTION STEPS:

- "Cheerleading" can start from within. Be your own cheerleader. Read *Daring Greatly* by Brené Brown, *Grit* by Angela Duckworth, and *Mindset* by Carol Dweck. These are powerful books that can inspire you to follow your dreams.
- Believe in yourself more than you believe what other people tell you is possible.

THIRTY-NINE

THERE'S ALWAYS SOMETHING BEHIND DOOR NUMBER THREE

In my coaching practice, I've noticed a crossroads where many clients find themselves. Whether just starting out in their career or a senior-level executive, newly married or awaiting their first grandchild, deciding to set out on a new adventure or stay where they are—there's often an either/or mindset. *Is this a yes or a no? Should I make this choice or should I make that choice?* Two options. That's it. They box themselves in and when neither alternative is ideal, they choose the lesser of two evils or become immobilized by "analysis paralysis" and make no decision at all.

As soon as you believe you have no choice in the matter, guess what? You don't. The moment you're convinced that your options are limited, you are absolutely right. At that point, your brain is locked. You've shut out any other possibilities because you don't even *believe* they exist. You've limited yourself. So the next time you're considering two possibilities and neither seems ideal, remember: *There's always something behind Door Number Three.*

When Alyssa, a journalism major, was in her junior year of college, she started looking into internship opportunities. She went to the career center on a mission: to secure an internship with either the ABC, CBS, or NBC news affiliate in Los Angeles. That seemed to be the most logical—and exciting—choice. After all, her ultimate goal was to be a television reporter. Unfortunately, as she researched the catalog of available internships for her major, television news was nowhere to be found. In the words of the college administrator, "That internship isn't available through—" Well, I'll omit the name of Alyssa's university. Fortunately, Alyssa wasn't one to take "no" for an answer. Doors Number One and Two were *related* to her major but not a straight line from where she was to where she wanted to be. Alyssa decided to knock on Door Number Three. She contacted Channel 2 News—the CBS affiliate—and found that she could apply directly, instead of through her school, and still receive college internship credits. Alyssa was thrilled! And even more so when Channel 2 News selected her to intern with the producer of its special series, doing research and conducting preliminary interviews.

Looking behind Door Number Three was a real confidence booster for Alyssa because she experienced firsthand how it looked and felt to make a bold move. She learned that she is not a passive recipient of circumstance. The experience also nudged her—inspired her—to creatively search out answers and opportunities that aligned with her vision.

Door Number Three is at every turn. I found it as I was completing this book. Just before securing a publishing contract, I attended the Kauai Writers Conference, which, by the way, I highly recommend for any aspiring authors out there. I went to Hawaii with four goals:

- Identify and implement strategies to help me build an author platform—check! (A big thank-you to Lisa Sharkey at HarperCollins.)
- Meet other like-minded authors and build a community of writers in which we provide each other with feedback, exchange ideas and resources,

> celebrate each other's successes, and yes, talk each
> other off the ledge when rejection and setbacks
> threaten to inhibit our muse—check!
>
> - Connect with at least one publisher who shows an
>   interest in my book and sees the value of getting it
>   out there—check! (Big shout out to Holly
>   Kammier at Acorn Publishing!)
> - Walk away from the conference 100 percent
>   certain of the publishing path I want to pursue
>   (traditional publishing or self-publishing)—check!
>   Well . . . sort of. That's where Door Number Three
>   comes in. But first, let me backtrack for a moment.

For years (more years than I care to mention), the dream had been to attract a top-tier literary agent who would then sell publishing rights to one of the Big Five publishing houses: Hachette, HarperCollins, Macmillan, Penguin Random House, and Simon & Schuster. While I was big on dreams and creative ideas to promote this book, I was lacking a platform, a following, a book-buying audience already in place, waiting —and then sprinting—to buy or even pre-order my book. This void lowered my chances of landing a traditional publishing deal. Significantly. In fact, for a debut nonfiction author, it was a deal-breaker. Agents had given me positive feedback on the writing but "would not be able to sell it without a platform." I was discouraged. *Very discouraged.* So much so that I spent over twenty years *not* writing this book. More accurately, it was a series of stops and starts—mostly stops. If I had a do-over, I would have spent less energy being disheartened and more energy exploring other avenues. I was so married to the idea of a traditional publisher that I couldn't see Door Number Three. Or even Door Number Two. Quite honestly, giving up on the dream of signing with a big New York publishing house felt like I was quitting, throwing in the literary towel, so to speak. But I eventually came to learn that sometimes the dream-come-true shows up where we least expect it.

Fast-forward, circa 2022. On the opposite end of the spectrum (Door Number Two), I had begun researching self-publishing, which offers complete creative control, 100 percent of the profits, and the potential for quicker book-to-market time, unencumbered by my lack of fame or social media following. The downside: In most cases, the author manages all aspects of the publishing process, including editing, distribution, book cover, interior design, and marketing. Additionally, there is absolutely no vetting process, so standards in the self-publishing world are all over the map.

I wanted to have creative control *and* the credibility that comes with a highly selective vetting process. It was also important to me that I work with a talented team and that my book be judged on literary merit—not my author platform. *Enter Door Number Three:* Signing with a reputable hybrid publisher with a track record of success.

Hybrid publishing has gained momentum in recent years, although I was only vaguely familiar with it and in some ways was completely misinformed. After attending the Kauai Writers Conference, I decided—with this book—the hybrid publishing model would offer the best of both worlds: higher royalties and more control than traditional publishing; greater support and distribution channels than self-publishing. If I had stayed in the either/or mindset, teetering between traditional publishing and self-publishing, I would not have found the best fit for me and the right home for my book behind Door Number Three.

ACTION STEPS:

- When you find yourself at an important crossroads, don't view it as a fork in the road.

That's far too limiting. Try this: Identify your goal, question, or quandary at the top of a page. Then write every possible idea to either bring the goal to fruition, answer the question, or overcome the challenge. Keep writing until you get to the bottom of the page. No cheating. Use a full $8\frac{1}{2}$" × 11" sheet of paper. Not an index card. Initially, the ideas will flow generously. Those last few, on the other hand, can be the hardest to land—and are often where your best ideas will surface. This exercise will get you thinking creatively outside the box, looking for—and being open to—Door Number Three. Remember, the possibilities are limited only by your imagination!

- Do the above exercise *regularly* and you'll become more creative and optimistic in your thinking. You will build your confidence muscle because you will see challenges and opportunities as being within your control. *You Got This!*

- Like Alyssa, *always ask the question.* If you don't, the answer will remain a "no" 100 percent of the time. By simply putting it out there, asking the question, and courageously opening Door Number Three, you've already increased your odds of a "yes" by 50 percent! I'm not a "bettin' man," but if I were, I'd say those are pretty good odds.

- Not making a decision *is* a decision. Get into action. Today.

FORTY

BECOME WISER WITHOUT LOSING YOUR INNOCENCE

As a teenager, I asked my father, "Why do older men always go for younger women?" After flashing me that familiar where-did-you-come-up-with-*that*-question-just-yesterday-you-were-in-diapers look, he said, "Sometimes when women get older, they lose a certain innocence."

I've always remembered his words. He wasn't referring to virginity, or naivete. He was talking about a fresh, optimistic, youthful outlook on life. An inner beauty filled with hope and wonder. Bright-eyed anticipation versus the negativity and hostility of a woman who has been hurt, betrayed, or disappointed one too many times. I get it. I suppose innocence attracts *all of us*, to a certain degree, because it transports us to a place and time when we looked only to the future. Never the past. Children personify innocence because they see the world through wide eyes and an open heart. To a child, life is an exciting adventure. Everything is ahead of them. They haven't lived long enough to harbor resentment. They haven't experienced enough to build walls.

With each passing year, life begets either bitterness or wisdom. And it's not a matter of circumstance. It's a choice. *You* get to decide how life's experiences are going to shape you.

Some time ago, I met a fellow author, Savannah, at a writer's conference. I was surprised to learn she was forty-one years old. I had her figured for twenty-seven-ish, not just because of her youthful looks but because she had this innocence that was very captivating. Savannah later shared with me a piece of her childhood. Among other things, she was physically abused. She hardly lived a charmed life and had every reason to be bitter. But where would that white-knuckle grip on the past have gotten her?

Instead, she abandoned bitterness and hatred and emerged as a stronger, more determined person. Savannah didn't deny, or sugarcoat, her past. That's not what I'm asking you to do. She faced, acknowledged, confronted, learned from, and made peace with the past. She relinquished the power it held over her. This allowed her to move on. In the end, those experiences actually gave her writing an edgy, more authentic voice.

Become wiser without losing your innocence. Learn from the bad without anticipating it. Grow from the disappointment without projecting it. Hope cannot coexist with anger, resentment, or despair.

My dad was right. Some women (and men) lose their innocence. It gets buried and crushed beneath layers of life. When hope feels too vulnerable, they trade it in for cynicism, all the while convincing themselves that they're stronger. Better. But that's only an *illusion* of strength. Strength comes, not by putting up barriers or by making people in the present pay for the sins of our past. The strength comes when we rise above our circumstances, when we learn from the shortcomings of ourselves and others, and when—in spite of our history, and because of it, we can still embrace life with discernment *and* the confident expectation of good. Only then can we become wiser without losing our innocence.

ACTION STEPS:

- Divide a piece of paper into six stacked columns—three on the top and three on the bottom.
  - In the upper left column, write one sentence that describes an experience that caused you to put your guard up—and how you felt in response to it. It will likely be something someone did (or did not do) to hurt, disappoint, or infuriate you. Be sure to "own" your feelings—for instance, say "I felt . . . " instead of "So-and-so made me feel . . . " Here are some examples: "I felt betrayed when I found out my boyfriend slept with my best friend." "I felt inadequate when my book proposal was rejected." "I was heartbroken when my parents divorced."
  - To the right, in the second column, describe your interpretation of that event. Using the example above—"I felt betrayed when I found out my boyfriend slept with my best friend"—your interpretation of that event might have been, "All men are cheaters. Men cannot be trusted!"
  - In the third column, write down your subsequent actions based on that interpretation. For example (and your reaction may differ), based on the interpretation "All men are cheaters; they cannot be trusted," your corresponding behavior might have been to avoid commitment. Or to sabotage your relationships. Or to be excessively jealous and suspicious. Perhaps even to cheat, preferring to be the deceiver instead of the deceived. *It's*

important to recognize that the behavior is there as a coping mechanism, helping you avoid reexperiencing those difficult emotions. So ask yourself, *Is this behavior working for me? Does it serve me well? Is it moving me closer to the person I want to become? Is my life better as a result of those behaviors? Or is it just safer?*

- ○ Now, in the lower left side of the page, *rewrite* (as originally stated in the first column) what happened and how you felt.

- In the next column, record what you learned from that experience. Again, these are just examples to prime the pump. Your number one takeaway may vary. Did you learn that if a person lacks integrity in one area, they may very likely lack integrity in other areas of life? Did you come to appreciate that when someone reveals their true character, you best believe them? After some reflection, did you realize that you gravitate toward the "players" and that you need to recalibrate your romantic barometer? Or maybe you came to the conclusion that early on in your relationships—especially if the guy is smokin' hot—you become so emotionally and physically invested that you tend to see your partner through "rose-colored glasses?"
  - ○ We are more likely to lose our innocence when we're feeling bitter and resentful. It's important to recognize that when we're in that headspace, we're looking outward. We're blaming someone. And yes, if you find your boyfriend in bed with your BFF, I, for one, can immediately think of two people who bear the blame! But remember, the goal is to become wiser *without losing your innocence.* When you explore what

you've learned—even though it may have been a difficult and painful lesson—you're looking inward. And looking forward. That perspective allows you to grow from the experience without becoming embittered by it.

- In that last column, describe how, based on your situation, you can become wiser without losing your innocence. For example, following the boyfriend/best friend theme, you may choose to allow the friendship with your partner to evolve at a faster rate than the physical side of the relationship. While keeping hopefully optimistic, this approach will give you a chance to see what he is made of, so you don't end up trusting someone who simply is not trustworthy. As discussed in other chapters, you can observe how he treats other people. *That's* how he will eventually treat you.

- Affirmations are a powerful way to shift your energy and align with what you want and who you are committed to becoming.
  - If you're struggling to become wiser without losing your innocence, repeat this affirmation —with conviction—several times each day: "While I choose to shine my light brightly, generously, and wholeheartedly on *everyone*, I only attract friends, clients, and romantic partners who—through their words and actions —appreciate and value my light."
  - Visualize how that outcome will look.
  - Feel the feeling of having it now.
  - Then, *act as if!*

FORTY-ONE

ACCOUNTABILITY MAKES NO EXCUSES

O kay, so you blew it. You said the wrong thing. You did the wrong thing. You mishandled a situation, either personally or professionally. We've all been there. The question is, what are you going to do about it? You can either let it go and pretend nothing ever happened, or you can step up to the plate. If you choose being responsible over being a weenie, congratulations. You're on the right track. But here's something you may not know—there are varying degrees of accountability. They are:

1. **None whatsoever**

If you want people to respect you, and if you want to respect yourself, this is not an option. When there's no ownership of wrong or hurtful behavior, one of two things is typically the underlying issue—an awareness *deficiency* . . . or a pride *surplus*. Some people have a complete personal blind spot. There's a total lack of self-awareness. More often than not, though, most people recognize when they've handled a situation poorly, or said something hurtful or inappropriate, but pride keeps them from admitting the transgression. *If I don't admit I'm wrong, they'll never know.* Guess what? They know! And not owning up to it doesn't diminish the offense. In fact, the opposite is true. It magnifies it.

2. **You admit what you did but make allowances for your behavior**

Example: *"Yes, I lied, but I wouldn't have had to if everyone weren't so judgmental."*

We'll never find answers when we're looking for excuses. The path of least resistance, of course, is to blame our problems and mistakes on other people. After all, that relinquishes us of responsibility. And embarrassment. We don't look quite as bad, or so we think. But excuses immobilize us. They keep us in a rut; a reactive, problem-focused, negative state of mind. Accountability, on the other hand, is proactive, solution-focused, action-oriented, and positive. Accountability makes no excuses, so it moves us forward in life. Own up to your mistakes without trying to justify them. People will like you more when you're not pointing fingers or rationalizing your actions. More importantly, *you'll like yourself more.*

3. **You admit it and apologize**

Example: *"I am so sorry I lied. I was afraid of being judged, but that's my problem, not yours."* This takes character and humility. People respect us when we "man up" and own up to our blunders. Apologizing is the first step toward mending a relationship, solving a problem, or overcoming a hurdle. And while saying "I'm sorry" is a start, it's not always enough. There are often times when we have to clean up the mess we left behind.

4. **You admit it, apologize, *and make restitution***

You may be thinking, *Hey, I acknowledged that I was wrong. I said I was sorry. Isn't that enough?* If you think that's sufficient, consider this: Someone just dumped fifty pounds of garbage in the middle of your living room. It's so dirty, so smelly, that even the *flies* are complaining about poor living conditions. The offender apologized profusely and promised she would never do it again. Well, that's just fine and dandy, but the bottom line is that there is *still* a week's worth of trash on your floor! She's not truly being accountable until she cleans it up. In other words, accept full responsibility for your actions by taking care of your "garbage," starting today. Level up. Own up. And clean up! Not doing so will negatively impact your relationships and your reputation and embed a pattern that will be difficult to reverse later in life. Continuing with the example above, restitution might mean circling back to others who were impacted by the lie and coming clean with the *real* story, especially if someone's reputation was damaged by the deception. Or, depending on the situation, financial compensation might be necessary in order to right the wrong.

There comes a point in time when we realize that our actions have consequences and we're willing to be responsible for them. It's called being a grown-up. The thing that distinguishes an adolescent from an adult is not chronology. It's maturity and accountability. Growing up isn't about hitting the milestones. It's all about what we do in between those milestones that counts.

ACTION STEPS:

- Have the right attitude. Humility, sincerity, and vulnerability beget humility, sincerity, and vulnerability. Replace excuses with ownership, and defensiveness will dissipate.

- "Extend an olive branch." Make plans to meet with your friend, your colleague, your family member, or with whomever you need to right the wrong.
- Check your ego at the door.
- Ask yourself, *Would I rather be right, or would I rather get results?* If your answer is, *I'd rather be right*, repeat the previous step: Check your ego at the door.
- Start your conversation with a heartfelt apology. And, by the way, "apologizing" that someone feels a certain way is only a *partial* apology! "I'm sorry you feel hurt" redirects some of the blame to *them*, whereas "I'm sorry I hurt you," takes full responsibility for what you said or did.
    - Without chronicling every detail of the mishap, be specific about where you went wrong.
    - Tell the person that you handled it poorly and "if I had a do-over," here's what I would do differently . . .
    - Acknowledge the impact your actions have had on the relationship.
    - Tell them what you've already done, or are doing, to rectify the situation and ask if there's anything else you can do to make things right.
    - Tell them you've "learned an important lesson," and relate your specific insights.
    - Finish your conversation by asking them to please accept your apology.
- With the right approach, tone, and intention, most people will receive your expression of regret with grace. If not, it's possible you either crossed a line of no return or the recipient of "I'm sorry" needs a little time to recover. If they *never* come around, at least you know you've done everything you could

to mend the relationship, and their refusal to let it go may be a sign that *they* are not a relationship worth holding on to.

YOUR GUT WILL SEE THINGS THAT YOUR INTELLECT MAY OVERLOOK

It was August 2012. Hot days, balmy nights. Weekend barbeques with friends and family, and fun-filled afternoons at the beach. For Michelle, only one thing made this summer different from any other: She couldn't wait for it to be over.

Ben, a family friend, was visiting for part of the summer. The guest room was situated just down the hall from the nursery. There was something unsettling about Ben being so close to her toddler, but Michelle's disquieting thoughts made absolutely no sense to her. She and her husband had known Ben for eight years and shared many mutual friends. He was kind to their daughter. Never did anything to cross the line. Still, Michelle couldn't sleep at night. She lay awake, inches from the baby monitor, watching, listening intently for suspicious sounds in the night. She vacillated between questioning *his* character and questioning her *own* fears. *Am I being paranoid? Where is this coming from? Am I feeling troubled or projecting because of what happened to me when I was a child?* Her head was spinning. On one hand, she was fiercely protective of her daughter. Yet she was also feeling guilty for imputing bad motives on a friend—one who had given her no cause for doubt. Intellectually, she had no reason to suspect him of inappropriate behavior. Yet she had this nagging feeling she couldn't ignore.

So the sleepless nights continued.

Fortunately, the summer passed without incident. Although Michelle still couldn't quite articulate why, she told her husband she didn't want Ben to stay with them again. She couldn't put her finger on it. It was just that little voice. Instinct. That feeling in the pit of her stomach.

Your gut will "see" things that your intellect may overlook. Logic operates on a conscious level, which means our brain is our ally only to the extent that it can recall past experiences that are relevant. Our gut—our body—on the other hand, stores *everything*: emotions, physical responses, sensory details. It kicks into high gear immediately, while our mind is still processing past and present.

Back to the story. Several years later, Michelle discovered Ben had a criminal record as a sex offender. A tidal wave of what-ifs came crashing through her head. Then a profound relief. Relief that nothing had happened. Relief that she wasn't crazy or that she wasn't being paranoid. Relief that she had listened to her gut and took precautionary measures—based not on evidence or logic, but on a physical reaction to someone who just didn't "feel" right in her home.

Trust your instincts. They may not make sense at the time. That's okay. They will eventually.

Your heart tells you what you *want* to do. Your head tells you what you *should* do. And your gut tells you what you *must* do. It points to true north. Your gut is that little voice that says big things. The next time it nudges you, listen carefully.

ACTION STEPS:

- Sometimes anxiety can masquerade as a gut instinct. So, for ninety days, keep a journal of people and situations your gut "sees." Record these instincts, along with your physical reactions, and subsequent decisions. Note how often your gut is correct.

- Your gut is like a well-trained conscience. The more you rely on it, listen to it, and follow it, the more responsive it becomes. The opposite is also true. If you ignore it, it loses its sensitivity and will no longer serve you. Listen to your gut, and with time, it will become more refined.

FORTY-THREE

WE SEE EXACTLY WHAT WE'RE LOOKING FOR

A few years ago, I purchased a Honda CR-V. Right after I bought the car—*and I mean immediately*—I couldn't believe how many CR-Vs were suddenly on the road. They were everywhere! So many more than a week, or even a day, prior.

Seriously, did Honda start manufacturing ten times as many CR-Vs the moment I drove off the lot?

Well . . . no.

So what accounted for the supposed increase? One, I had a greater awareness. Two, I was excited about the car, so I spotted others like it more easily. And three, something I call Intentional Perspective: We see *exactly* what we are looking for. And not just with cars. Intentional Perspective plays out in relationships. It shows up at work. And it determines whether the next big thing is a blip on our radar, or simply an undetected opportunity.

Knowledge and skills are learned. Intentional Perspective, on the other hand, is a mindset—something we have or do not have, based only on our *decision* to have it or not have it. Anyone—regardless of age, education, or skillset can apply Intentional Perspective in their lives. And it's as easy as adjusting the side-view mirrors on your car. In fact, metaphorically speaking, that's exactly what it is. You decide the angle you want to capture. It's entirely your call. If you're looking for the good in people, you're going to *see* it. If you're searching for the blessings in life, you'll *find* them. And if you are open to great opportunities, you will *recognize* them.

Maybe you know someone who wakes up most days expecting good things to happen and the right people to show up. Before dismissing them as "annoying," "overly perky," or "clearly indulging in illegal substances," consider that their outlook is usually a self-fulfilling prophecy. In a good way. They typically see and attract the right people and the ideal circumstances. That's not to say there aren't any bumps in the road. (Sorry, I couldn't resist the metaphor.) But the obstacles aren't the focal point, so they navigate them more gracefully.

Milking the car analogy, if your "mirror" is set to negativity, you will see plenty of it. Guaranteed. It's out there. But if you choose to make that your *focus*, you've got to know you're paying a high price for that outlook. Toxic relationships and a woe-is-me attitude will drain you. Don't give your power away! Adjust your Intentional Perspective to positivity and you'll find that negative people and disappointing circumstances will land in your "blind spot." Yes, they're still there, and your "peripheral vision" may catch them . . . which means you'll still learn something from the experience. But, to your credit, you won't become preoccupied with people and situations that zap your energy.

Intentional Perspective in Relationships

Confirmation bias is the tendency to interpret information in a way that aligns with our preexisting beliefs, values, and opinions. It's human nature. More often than not, people will look for evidence that suggests they were right about something or someone. So if you're telling yourself that people will invariably let you down, you will find validation to support that narrative. If you think no one is there for you, you will see situations corroborating that. On the other hand, if you know that you are loved and valued, that your tribe has your best interests at heart, your Intentional Perspective and internal narrative will be much more favorable. And so will your relationships. You'll see that your friends and family *have* rallied around you—even if it looks different from the set-in-stone, picture-perfect template you've constructed in your mind.

Let's look at a potential scenario. Imagine you have a good support system—friends and family who have been there for you, providing emotional and practical support. And let's say this has been fairly consistent. But what if someone in your inner circle does not offer support at every turn, or in the way you're expecting? Your Intentional Perspective will dictate how you choose to process and interpret these misses. If you expect people to disappoint, you'll end up *seeing exactly what you are looking for*. If you focus on what's lacking—rather than the many things for which you have to be grateful—you'll alienate the people in your life. This will trigger a downward spiral and, ironically, perpetuate the very situation you fear most: no one being there for you!

What about romantic relationships? If you were previously in a relationship with someone who cheated, you're probably going to get jealous or feel suspicious more easily than someone whose ex was faithful. Is your Intentional Perspective unfairly condemning an innocent person? On the other hand, looking for, and acknowledging, the things you appreciate in your partner will prompt more to be grateful for. What is recognized is repeated.

Intentional Perspective at Work

At work, when your "mirror" is adjusted toward innovation, you foster an environment of open communication, collaboration, and creativity—core values of highly effective teams. When your Intentional Perspective is set on team growth rather than individual gain, both the organization and the individual benefit. The reverse does not produce the same outcome.

When your Intentional Perspective is focused on inclusivity, you'll appreciate each person's uniqueness rather than find fault or cast aside people you may perceive as different. By doing so, you'll build bridges instead of walls. You'll discover that—as a human race—we have more similarities than differences. You'll become a person who garners respect. People will see you as a leader, with or without the title.

Intentional Perspective When Opportunity Knocks

Sara Blakely, founder and owner of the shapewear brand Spanx, applied Intentional Perspective to the tune of a $1.2 billion company that has literally transformed the way women look and feel. Adorned in white pants, open-toed shoes, and driven by a desire for a slimmer, smoother-looking appearance, she got the idea for Spanx "as a frustrated consumer" in 1998. She cut off the feet of her control top pantyhose to make her first pair of shapewear. Whereas many might have dismissed this unprecedented discovery, Blakely did not. This was a blip on her radar. A blip that she paid attention to! She recognized the opportunity immediately because, in her words, she "had already set the intention." (And aren't we grateful!) In 2012, Blakely became the world's youngest female self-made billionaire and made *Time* magazine's "*Time* 100" list of the one hundred most influential people in the world. In 2014, Forbes listed her as the ninety-third most powerful woman in the world. And at the time of publication, Spanx remains a prominent player in the shapewear market.

Intentional Perspective can work *for* us and it can work

against us. If we want to use it to attract what we want and not what we don't want, we have to first recognize that we have control over it. We have *total* control over it. Then—like anything else in life—we'll need to practice in order to get better. That means intentionally being open to, looking for, and moving toward what we want instead of what we don't want. You may be thinking, *Of course I'm open to what I want. Why wouldn't I be open to what I want?* Fair enough. But ask yourself how much time you spend doubting that "it" (whatever your "it" may be) will actually happen? Have you ever set a goal only to say, *Yeah right. If only. Who am I kidding?*

Intentional Perspective is simple. But it's not easy. Simple, because it's straightforward and uncomplicated. Not easy, because it takes discipline.

Adjust the mirror and you'll change the perspective. Then, and only then, will the people, circumstances, and opportunities you *see* align with the people, circumstances and opportunities you truly *want*.

ACTION STEPS:

- Identify one area in your life in which applying Intentional Perspective will have the greatest impact. Make a commitment to have Intentional Perspective in that specific area for thirty days. Be consistent.
- What were your insights and key takeaways? Any aha moments? What did you "see" differently this time around? In what ways has "adjusting the mirror" improved your outlook on life?

FORTY-FOUR

"HAVING IT ALL" COMES IN STAGES

I t probably started around the age of three: *When I grow up I'm going to be . . .* You matter-of-factly filled in the blank with your life's ambition. If your parents were like mine, they responded with something like, "You can do anything you want to do as long as you put your mind to it!" So, at the age of three—armed with encouragement, determination, and pint-sized attitude—I had it all figured out: I was going to be a famous movie star *and* the best mommy in the whole wide world. In short, I wanted (like every three-year-old) to have it all!

Through the years, I've come to realize that "having it all" comes in stages. With focus, determination, and consistent effort, we *can* have it all—but not necessarily at the same time. Something, or someone, will suffer. Our marriage. Our career. Our education. The relationship with our children. While the "having it all" quandary can play itself out in a variety of situations, I've seen the greatest push and pull between career and motherhood. The drive to succeed professionally and the desire to nurture a close-knit, loving family will inevitably battle it out. With any competition, there's either a tie, in which both sides feel a little cheated, or there is a clear winner—and an equally apparent loser. Yet we fool ourselves into thinking that life is one big juggling act. It isn't. A successful, high-profile, in-the-limelight career requires 100 percent commitment. So does raising children. And you can only slice up a pie so many times before it starts crumbling.

The concept of having it all is so deeply ingrained in us that it has become difficult to question its validity. Choosing between rising to the top of our field or being a full-time wife and mother will probably raise a few eyebrows, as if being singularly focused renders us "less than." That's not to say we can't pursue our dream *and* be a great mom. We can. We can devote quality time to more than one thing. Here is the factor that tips the scales: *When each goal requires enormous amounts of time, dedication, and energy, at least one of those commitments is going to require sacrifice.* Everyone would be better served (including ourselves) if we put something on hold—or took baby steps—while we focus on what is most important *at that particular point in time.*

If you want your family to have the biggest piece of the pie and you're tired of burning the candle at both ends, wondering what you're doing wrong, I'm here to tell you that you are doing *nothing* wrong. Having it all at the same time is a fallacy. It's okay to put your career on pause or at half speed while your kids are little. That may look like scaling back your hours if you have the means of doing so. It might mean switching to a less stressful job, so that you're more present when you are with your kids.

Having it all comes in stages. This lesson didn't come easy for me. After all, I grew up with the notion that "I could do anything I put my mind to," and if I put my mind to "having it all," well then, that was certainly fair game. Right? But in life there are trade-offs, and I had to consider the potential consequences of not giving my family priority.

When we're facing difficult choices, it helps to look beyond the immediate future. So ask yourself, *How will this decision affect my life five years from now? Ten years from now? In twenty years? Person-ally* (and I use that word intentionally, knowing what worked for me may not be the best choice for every woman out there), I didn't want to be wishing for a parenting do-over. I knew that when my children were grown, I wanted to be able to look back on a plethora of memories and experiences with them. From that vantage point, *my* answer was clear: Having it all would come with a price—one I wasn't willing to pay. My kids would only be little once. I could never recapture those impressionable years. And priceless moments don't come with an encore. I wanted to be there for that first step. I wanted to hear that first word. I wanted to experience that simultaneous look of shock, wonder, and sheer joy as they tasted ice cream for the first time. And of course, I wanted to see their inno-cent, hopeful eyes light up when they said, "Mommy, when I grow up, I'm going to be . . ."

ACTION STEPS:

- Write out a Personal Manifesto—a declaration of what you want in life. Use present tense language like, "I am . . ." and "I have . . ." Whatever follows that, the subconscious mind accepts as fact.
  - As you read the Manifesto, determine the *current* priority, based on your core values.
  - Just because "having it all" comes in stages, doesn't mean you can't focus most of your time and energy on the current priority while taking baby steps toward other aspirations. Set yourself up for the next "stage." For example, if you have a two-year-old-old daughter and you want to be a stay-at-home mom during her formative years but aspire to be a registered nurse, can you research nursing programs that

offer flexible schedules? Are you able to take online prerequisites? How about turning studying into a fun, interactive, family activity? For example, creating anatomy flashcards or simple games that you can play together. Taking actionable steps now will help you transition into that future stage more seamlessly—and with greater confidence—when the timing is right.

FORTY-FIVE

THE CELEBRATION PLATE

As my kids were growing up, there were a few things my family could count on at dinnertime: a home-cooked meal (well, *most* of the time), me scrambling to get dinner on the table by six o'clock-ish (I have a warped relationship with time), and the Celebration Plate. Each night, the Celebration Plate went to the person who had something especially good happen to them that day. It could be anything—acing a test, meeting someone new, achieving a personal or professional accomplishment, overcoming a challenge, having a great time with a good friend, going on a fun adventure. There were no rules. No boundaries.

So every night, with a smile and an anticipatory expression on my face, I made the rounds. "Okay, who gets the Celebration Plate tonight? What's the best thing that happened to *you* today?" Depending on each person's day, their attitude at that moment, and their hunger quotient, my questions were either met with a grin (*I think I deserve the Celebration Plate tonight*), complete indifference, or a roll of the eyes that practically begged, *Please take your inner Mister Rogers down a notch or two. It's been a rough day. I'm not in the mood for your enthusiasm! And I'm definitely not in the mood for the Celebration Plate!*

One day, I heard a more emphatic response: "*Nothing* good happened to *me* today!" My then sixteen-year-old daughter, Madison, countered, "Something good happens *every* day. We just have to look for it."

Wow! She has been listening all these years. After logging hours of second-guessing myself and wondering, *Is anything I'm saying sinking in*, I was savoring the moment!

Rewind, circa 2009. Madison and I are having a conversation about *choosing* to be happy. At the infinitely wise age of twelve, she has it all figured out: Good things + you = being happy. Bad things + you = being sad. Always the math wizard, she's certain her equation is spot-on. The concept of *choosing* to be happy is foreign to her. In her mind, it's all about cause and effect. "Not necessarily," I explain. "Our situation doesn't have to influence our happiness; our happiness can influence our situation, or at least the way we *view the situation*."

As we explored in a previous chapter, we see *exactly* what we're looking for. When we make a conscious decision to be grateful, we see all the things that bring us happiness—experiences, lessons, and people. Small, great things that are visible because we haven't allowed them to be eclipsed by our negative *interpretation* of a particular event. When we search for the good, obstacles are seen as beatable challenges. People are humanized, understood, and forgiven. The lens through which we look at life is either enhanced or tainted by our attitude. And our attitude . . . well, *that* determines whether we're living a life worth celebrating.

ACTION STEPS:

- Develop an attitude of gratitude. It's impossible for our mind to focus on both a positive and negative thought at the exact same time. Being more mindful of who and what we appreciate will help flush out negativity. This doesn't necessarily make the bad situation go away, but getting in a more optimistic headspace gives us a greater sense of control over our lives, changes the way we show up in the world, and allows us to have a greater impact on the people around us. So make it a goal to find two things to "celebrate" every day. I keep a gratitude journal. Right before going to bed, I write down two things I'm grateful for. Some days, the gratitude flows. On days when I might be tempted to think, "*Nothing* good happened today," I remind myself to refocus on the things I never want to take for granted—I have two arms to hold the people I love; I can pray and worship freely without the threat of being beaten or imprisoned; I have a roof over my head; and (something I'm coming to terms with) I'm a day older—which is a *good* thing. It means I'm here. I'm alive. If you're still not feeling the positivity vibe, ask yourself: *If I woke up tomorrow morning with only the people and things that I expressed gratitude for today, what would I have?*

- Despite your resolute efforts to maintain an attitude of gratitude, you're human. Even if you're superhuman, negative thoughts will creep in from time to time. Don't discount them. What you resist, persists. So, before you can rock that superwoman cape and fully own *You Got This!*, first acknowledge those negative thoughts. Thank them for sharing. Give them a voice. And this next part is important: When you verbalize the negative thought, insert the phrase, "Right now, it feels like . . ." or "Right now, it feels as if . . ." So instead of saying, "My life is falling apart," say, "*Right now, it feels like* my life is falling apart." Or after a bad breakup, rather than "I'll never find love again," say, "*Right now, it feels as if* I'll never find love again." Adding the qualifier makes the statement questionable—and more manageable—instead of indisputable.

- After acknowledging, perform Mental CPR.
  - **C—Challenge the negative thought.** This reduces the emotional charge by putting distance and perspective between you and the situation. Ask yourself, *Is it really true that . . .?* and insert the negative thought, questioning its validity. Probe deeper with questions like, *Am I magnifying the negative? Is this a pattern with me?* If so, in the words of Dr. Phil, *How's that working for you?* It's very difficult to reverse negative thinking without first challenging its validity. Once you've done that, you're ready for the next step.
  - **P—Ponder another perspective.** Look for evidence to support a different viewpoint. If a disagreement with someone triggered your negative thinking, consider the other person's point of view. If you're experiencing a defeatist attitude as a result of negative self-talk, remind yourself of previous wins, successes, and proud moments. Don't fall into the trap of confusing the facts *with your interpretation of the facts.*
  - **R—Reframe the negative thought.** The idea here is not to change or manipulate what's at the heart of the issue. The goal is to reframe your thought in such a way that you shift your perspective from reactive to proactive, negative to positive, and problem-oriented to solution-oriented.
  - Using the Acknowledge + Mental CPR framework, here's an example: Let's say you

come home at the end of the day and you're feeling completely overwhelmed. The soundtrack playing in your head is, "I'm never going to meet all these deadlines!"

- **Validate:** *"It feels as if* I'm never going to meet all these deadlines."

  - **C—Challenge** the negative thought: *Is it really true that I'll never meet all these deadlines? Or am I just feeling so tired and overwhelmed that I'm not able to see my way clearly?*

  - **P—Ponder** another perspective: Reflect on past experiences and think of one or more times when you felt buried and actually accomplished everything by the deadline. Or identify a situation when you reprioritized, you accomplished *the most important things*, and all the stakeholders were satisfied. That's your evidence that you can do it again! So ask yourself, *What did I do to contribute to either of those outcomes? And in what ways did I show up differently in order to accomplish those goals?* Depending on the situation, **pondering another perspective** can include thinking outside the box, leveraging your resources, and getting creative!

  - **R—Reframe** the negative thought from "It feels as if I'm never going to meet all these deadlines" to "What task or project can I tackle first that will either streamline the remaining tasks or make them less daunting?" Again, the goal of the reframe is to shift the perspective from reactive to proactive, negative to positive, and/or problem-oriented to solution-oriented. You know you've landed a compelling reframe when your emotions shift and you start moving forward instead of remaining at a standstill.

FORTY-SIX

———————

BE THE SUN

Daniel was a bit stiff. Not nervous stiff. Or robotic stiff. But he gave off this aloof vibe that lowered his relatability factor. Significantly. This, combined with his good looks and confident, slightly out-of-reach demeanor, made people admire him from afar but not necessarily gravitate toward him to introduce themselves.

As an asset and portfolio manager, he knew this was a barrier, so he hired me as his coach. The goal: to become more effective, relatable, and influential when giving presentations to existing and prospective clients.

Fortunately, I had experienced the *other* Daniel. The Daniel who is warm and authentic. I knew if his clients saw that side of him, his business would thrive.

According to Dale Carnegie & Associates, a global training and development company, people admire us for what we have, respect us for what we do, *but they will only trust us for who we are.* And Daniel wasn't revealing who he was.

We were fifteen minutes into a presentation coaching session when I reminded him, "Daniel, loosen up. Smile. You look more relatable and approachable when you do. All things being equal, people do business with people they like. Let your personality show."

"I'm concerned that I won't look professional," he countered.

"*Are* you professional?"

"Of course."

"If you're *already* professional then why do you have to *try* to look professional?"

Momentarily stumped by the irony of my question, I took advantage of the opportunity and walked over to his wall-to-wall window overlooking the California coast. The afternoon sun popped against a cloudless blue backdrop and I asked, "Is the sun bright?"

"Yes."

"Does the sun have to *try* to be bright?

"No."

"Is the sun warm?"

"Yes," he grinned, sensing where I was going with this.

"Does the sun have to *try* to be warm?"

"No."

"Daniel, you're confident. You're professional. You're knowledgeable," I reminded him. "That's who you are. You don't have to *try* to be those things. When you do, you over-compensate, and it just doesn't serve you. It's not coming across as real. And if you don't come across as real, people aren't going to trust you with their money."

He was beginning to connect the dots when I added, "Be the sun! The sun doesn't have to try to be bright or warm or cheery. It just is. *Be* who you already are. Don't *try*."

That's when the light bulb went on. As Daniel was striving to be something he already was (professional), he was appearing to be something he wasn't (insincere). Once he embraced the "Be the sun" mindset, he was able to build greater trust with clients and forge stronger connections with colleagues and prospects. As a result, his business began to grow. People were then drawn to—and engaged by—his balance of credibility and relatability. It was natural. Organic. Not something he had to force.

How often do we find ourselves in Daniel's predicament—in business, in personal relationships, and in unfamiliar social situations—wanting to project a certain image? Have we found ourselves trying too hard? When that happens, it backfires. We miss opportunities, we make mediocre impressions, and we fail to get the results we're looking for because people sense inauthenticity faster than a bloodhound can sniff out the perpetrator in a murder mystery novel.

After coaching thousands of people over the last fifteen years, I've noticed a common theme among women in their twenties and thirties: a compulsion to prove themselves, especially in a male-dominated work environment. Even saying it out loud—"I have to prove my value"—feels heavy. And while that statement might kick-start your resolve, that's a lot of weight to carry around. Instead, try on, "I want to *share* my value." Just the sound of that evokes different emotions and, by extension, different behaviors.

Be the sun! Relatability and credibility are not mutually exclusive. In fact, relatability *enhances* our credibility, because in the absence of relatability, trust will not survive.

ACTION STEPS:

- Picture a circumstance in which your knee-jerk response would be to try to prove yourself. For example, this could be a job interview, a first date, meeting the family and longtime friends of your significant other, or any scenario where there is self-imposed pressure to shine. Imagine that the desired result was *already* a done deal: You landed the job. The date was a success. Your partner's friends and family loved you, and so on. *Now, let's reverse engineer and act as if.* How would you present yourself in an interview, for example, if you knew you were getting the job? For starters, you would likely be enthusiastic, eager to share your value. You would come across confident instead of overconfident, insecure, or desperate, because there would be nothing you had to prove. You would be sincerely interested in your new colleagues; that authenticity and personal interest would come across and possibly position you as a good fit, culturally. *Act as if.*

- Don't *prove* your value. Come from a place of generosity and *share* your value.
- Be yourself! Everyone else is taken. *You Got This!*

SOME FINAL WORDS

I hope you've enjoyed *You Got This! Honest Lessons on Life, Love, and Leveling Up*. Time is our most valuable resource, so I feel honored and humbled that you've spent this time with me, through the pages of this book.

As you reflect on these life lessons, think about what resonated most with you. Where did you see yourself, your friends, and your family? I encourage you to open up the conversation with the people in your life. Collectively doing so will help us all reclaim and rebuild our village.

Whether you're a personal development junkie or just getting started, you have the power to level up and create your future. As author and motivational speaker Darren Hardy says, "Stop waiting for someone or something to light your fire. *You* have the match." As you're blazing your trail, here are some thoughts to keep in mind:

- Let your missteps *refine* you. Don't let them *define* you. A self-imposed label can be difficult to remove.
- Don't look back unless that's the direction you want to go . . . or at least just look back long

enough to learn the lesson. Then *move* forward. *And pay it forward.* The more we grow, the more we have to give.

- Embrace your journey and empower others. Who can you adopt, so to speak, as a little sister? Who can you champion and mentor?
- Each day, become a better version of you. Perfection is not required. In fact, perfection is overrated. And it doesn't exist. We are all a work in progress. I know I am. I hope I always will be. Because the day I stop learning and growing is the day something inside of me dies.

As I shared with you in the introduction, the idea for this book came to me when my daughter, Madison, was a baby. I wanted her to have the benefit of everything I did the "right" way, as well as the benefit of lessons learned along the way. Individually, and as a society, we innately want to pass our wisdom and experience on to those who follow. My advice to you? Make the right choices *today* so you don't regret the wrong choices *tomorrow.* Sure, we all learn from mistakes. But now, those mistakes don't have to be *yours.* What began as a mother's wish and intention for her daughter has expanded to include women around the globe—I hope you make the best choices I *ever* made . . . and the best choices I *never* made.

ACKNOWLEDGMENTS

Writing this book has been a labor of love, and it would not have been possible without the support of so many incredible people.

My deepest thanks to my husband, Mark, whose dedication and work ethic have anchored our family for more than three decades. Thank you for your support as I raised our kids, worked part-time around their schedules, and built this next chapter in my life. You carried the heavier financial load so I could put family first while still contributing in my own way—a balance I'll always be grateful for. You've been a faithful husband, a devoted father, and the steady hand that has always kept our family grounded. I could not have written this without the solid foundation you built for us.

Madison and Michael, being your mom has been the greatest joy of my life! It's shaped me into a better person—more compassionate, more loving, more insightful, more patient. Motherhood has refined me in ways I never expected, and because of that, I've been able to write from a deeper, more wholehearted place. So, in many ways, you've both contributed to this book more than you realize. I love you to the moon and stars and back a million gazillion times. (No, you're not too old for me to say it. And yes, I'm crying. No surprise there.)

Daddy, my heart has always been so closely connected to yours that it's hard to imagine it beating without you. Thank you for instilling in me a deep love of the written word. And thank you for always believing in me. You've given me enough encouragement to last an eternity.

To my mom, who passed away in 2019, I miss you. I miss your sparkle and your moxie. I wish you were here to share this moment with me. I think you would be really proud of this book. Proud of me. Thank you for raising me to be a woman of integrity. To speak up and take a stand for what I believe in.

A heartfelt thank-you to my "bonus" parents, Pat and Bill. Not everyone is fortunate enough to truly love the people their divorced parents remarry, and I never take that blessing for granted. Pat, thank you for loving Daddy. Bill, thank you for loving Mommy. I appreciate you both for always being there for the kids you inherited. You've never felt like stepparents—*always the real thing.*

I'm grateful to have the ongoing love and support of my siblings—Frankie, Traci, Bobby, Saretta, and Jonika. I expressed your awesomeness in chapter 28, so I'll keep it short and sweet: You're the best! I can't imagine having gone through this life without you.

To my tribe of friends and extended family who have cheered me on, believed in me when I doubted myself, and reminded me to keep going—you know who you are—you mean the world to me! Thank you for being my people. I feel so blessed to have you in my life!

I'm very thankful for the expertise of my editor, Marci Clark. You helped me approach certain sections with greater sensitivity and encouraged me to add more detail and depth where the stories *and readers* needed it. Your insights made this book more relatable and authentic, and I'm so grateful for your advice throughout the process. Thank you for helping me "level up" as an author.

Bringing a book into the world is never a solo act. I'm thankful to the team at Acorn Publishing for your support and guidance in helping turn my dream into a reality—including copublishers Holly Kammier and Jessica Therrien, and the talented team of Lily Anderson, Leslie Ferguson, Cody Raschella, Kat Ross, Nico Seidita, and Kayla Toris. Yay! We did it! Thank you to Susie Schaefer for helping me navigate the ins and outs of getting my book to truly stand out on Amazon. To the design team at Damonza, thank you for crafting a cover that reflects the energy and optimism behind *You Got This!* Each of you has played a part in bringing *You Got This!* to life, and I'm grateful for your belief in this book and in me.

A heartfelt thank-you to my publishing coordinator, Jessica Hammett, whose steady presence, thoughtful communication, and encouragement helped me navigate every step of the process. You've been exceptional not just because of what you do and how you do it but because of who you are—passionate, enthusiastic, and deeply committed. I've felt your support every step of the way. You've been an anchor in the whirlwind, and I'm truly grateful.

I also want to thank Viviana Schilpp, LCSW, for sharing your professional insight and compassionate perspective. Your advice helped me approach a few emotionally charged subjects with more balance and empathy. On a broader scope, thank you for the meaningful work you do to help people heal, grow, and reclaim their strength.

A special thank you to my daughter, Madison, for your candid feedback and savvy insights as I refined this manuscript. You helped me see the work through the eyes of the readers I most wanted to reach, and your perspective made this stronger and more relatable. You inspired this book when you were just a baby and having you offer feedback on the gift I wrote for you was one of the most meaningful full-circle moments of my life.

To my coaches Michaelann Christ, Perception Repatterning Technique™ (PRT™) Practitioner, and Debi Delaney, Repatterning Practitioner, thank you for helping me clear creative blocks and get out of my own way. Your guidance at some pivotal points made it easier to refocus, push through, and keep moving forward.

A note of appreciation to Ross Hartmann and the team at Kiingo AI, who showed me how to use AI as a creative marketing tool for *You Got This!*, and to Haley Grace McCormick and Ivy Perry for getting my social media efforts started. Your support shaped the foundation for what's still to come. And to my photographer, Cindy Neal of Cindy Lynn Portrait, thank you for capturing the joy!

To the authors and thought leaders who have inspired me —thank you. Your words have changed lives and given others a voice. Sara Blakely, you remind us that when we help a woman fulfill her potential, magic happens. Brené Brown, thank you for breathing new life into "the man in the arena" and for your work on courage and vulnerability. Amy Cuddy, your power pose has become part of my prewriting ritual. Jess Ekstrom, thank you for helping women amplify their voices. Jefferson Fisher, you make communication feel both strong and kind—bravo! Marie Forleo, "everything is figureoutable" plays on repeat in my head. Mel Robbins, "let them" has been a game changer. And Reese Witherspoon, thank you for championing stories that put women front and center. I hope to thank you all in person someday.

I owe a debt of gratitude to the women who shared their stories with me—and had the courage to speak about experiences that weren't easy to revisit. Thank you for doing it scared. Your honesty and vulnerability will help others feel seen.

And finally, to every reader who picks up this book—thank you for trusting me with your time and your heart. My hope is that these pages help you believe in your own strength a little more. *You Got This!* And I mean that from the bottom of my heart.

ABOUT THE AUTHOR

Lisa Bartley is an author and award-winning speaker who helps women break free from their comfort zones and step into the strongest, truest versions of themselves.

You Got This! began as an attempt to record words of wisdom she wishes she'd heard in her early adult years. Now, in its completion, it stands as a legacy of lessons written for her daughter and for every young woman finding her way.

Lisa lives in Southern California where she prefers her hikes coastal, her wine bold, and her dinner parties unforgettable.